CHAPTER ONE

# EDITOR'S PICKS

## Salcombe

**EDITOR'S PICKS** | **FOR MORE INFO, SEE P11** |

Salcombe is one of Devon's most picturesque harbour towns, with views over the crystal clear water. Dolphins and a multitude of fishing boats call this scenic location home. Houses in an array of pastel tones form the backdrop, which sits close to the mouth of the sparkling Salcombe-Kingsbridge Estuary.

## Beer Beach

**EDITOR'S PICKS** | **FOR MORE INFO, SEE P13** |

Situated in the picture postcard fishing village of Beer, this sweeping shingle beach is enveloped by vertiginous limestone cliffs. Believed to have once been a preferred location for smugglers, fisherman today regularly launch their boats from the shore.

2

## Canonteign Falls

**EDITOR'S PICKS** | **FOR MORE INFO, SEE P20** |

Canonteign is home to some of England's most spectacular waterfalls: both the natural falls created over the centuries in this valley and the picturesque falls named after the 3rd Lady Exmouth and built under her direction in 1890. The falls provide inspiration for many photographers and painters due to their striking beauty.

3

## Corfe Castle

**EDITOR'S PICKS** | **FOR MORE INFO, SEE P168**|

Guarding the principal route through the Purbeck Hills, the 1000 year old Corfe Castle's dramatic remains stand in an elevated position as a representation of its colourful and significant history. The tumbledown, moss embellished walls and rugged beauty conceal its diverse and often turbulent past.

4

## Stoned

**EDITOR'S PICKS** | **FOR MORE INFO, SEE P86** |

Stoned pizza house is the original entrepreneurial concept from a young 16 year old who set out in 2013 touring campsites and pop-ups with a wood-fired pizza oven in tow. They specialise in stone baked foods, which have become a huge hit and resulted in this popular restaurant in Braunton.

## The Thirsty Bird

**EDITOR'S PICKS** | **FOR MORE INFO, SEE P106** |

The Thirsty Bird is a relaxed and beautifully designed café serving speciality coffee, delicious cheeses and charcuterie alongside a decent wine menu. They believe in serving quality produce, whilst creating a welcoming, friendly atmosphere where you can truly relax and take some time out.

## Durdle Door

**EDITOR'S PICKS** | **FOR MORE INFO, SEE P12** |

The magnificent geological wonder, Durdle Door is a limestone arch rising out of the aquamarine water at 200ft high, along the Jurassic Coast. As part of the World Heritage Site, the arch is also part of the Lulworth Estate and a short walk from Lulworth Cove.

## Ryder & Hope

**EDITOR'S PICKS** | **FOR MORE INFO, SEE P138**|

Ryder & Hope is an interesting design led collaboration incorporating interiors, retail and online. The brand encompasses an interior design service that focuses on commercial properties as well as domestic spaces. Ryder & Hope Store is their first retail space, selecting products from designers and crafts people as well as finding pieces to inspire everyday living.

8

## ODE True Food

**EDITOR'S PICKS** | **FOR MORE INFO, SEE P78** |

Café Ode is renowned for its sustainable approach to using quality, ethical and seasonal ingredients in a family friendly environment. Architecturally the café was created from the original Ness stables and is considered a fusion of art renovation, conversion and new sustainable build.

## The Station Kitchen

**EDITOR'S PICKS** | **FOR MORE INFO, SEE P83** |

Situated on the edge of the Old West Bay Station platform, The Station Kitchen showcases the best of Dorset's produce from its fresh catch, succulent local meat and garden grown vegetables, cleverly fusing old world charm with contemporary culinary excellence.

## Lynmouth Cliff Railway

**EDITOR'S PICKS** | **FOR MORE INFO, SEE P38** |

Lynton and Lynmouth are two historic towns whose economic and tourist development were being significantly hampered by the 500ft cliffs which separated them in the 19th century. Over 125 years old, this funicular solved that problem and once built became the steepest in the world.

## Riverford Field Kitchen

**EDITOR'S PICKS** | **FOR MORE INFO, SEE P79** |

Surrounded by acres of organic fruit and veg and a busy working farm is Riverford Field Kitchen. An open barn that blends into the countryside, filled with long tables and a mass of colour on the walls from drying flowers.

## Annie and the Flint

**EDITOR'S PICKS** | **FOR MORE INFO, SEE P118**

Exposed, whitewashed bricks, fresh flowers and soft grey paintwork create the interior style of Annie and the Flint café in Ilfracombe. Furnished with vintage travel trunks and leather armchairs, the café offers delicious cakes served with coffee and papers in a relaxed, ambient setting.

## Putsborough Beach

**EDITOR'S PICKS** | **FOR MORE INFO, SEE P39** |

Putsborough Sands is a sweeping golden sand beach, lapped by the Atlantic, to form the southern section of Woolacombe Sands. Close to the Baggy Point headland which provides the beach with a little shelter, the waters are popular with surfers, particularly long boarders.

## nkuku lifestyle store

**EDITOR'S PICKS** | **FOR MORE INFO, SEE P132**

nkuku is one of a kind and sources some of the most attractive lifestyle and home-ware products in the UK. The buyers work with artisans throughout the world bringing stylish and beautiful furnishings back to their barn in Devon.

## Rockets and Rascals

**EDITOR'S PICKS** | **FOR MORE INFO, SEE P122**

Rockets and Rascals is the perfect venue for all things related to cycling. Opened in the spring of 2013, with a mission to get people riding bikes, they are now Plymouth's only award winning bicycle shop, and in 2014 opened their second emporium in Poole.

16

## The Seaside Boarding House

**EDITOR'S PICKS** | **FOR MORE INFO, SEE P71** |

The Seaside Boarding House overlooks the sand-coloured cliffs of Hive Beach and beyond to the majestic arm of "The Chesil". This bright restaurant looks out over the ocean, with French windows opening onto a wide terrace, where diners can enjoy the flavours of the coast accompanied by a sea breeze.

17

## Yellow Bicycle Café

**EDITOR'S PICKS** | **FOR MORE INFO, SEE P130**

With a bicycle inspired decor, Yellow Bicycle Cafe is a contemporary spot in the heart of Blandford Forum. Popular for its innovative menu, using fresh, high quality local ingredients, their artisanal coffee and their home-baked bread is also a hit.

18

## Royal Albert Memorial Museum

**EDITOR'S PICKS** | **FOR MORE INFO, SEE P165**

The Royal Albert Memorial Museum holds a diverse collection of over 1 million objects including examples of zoology, anthropology, fine art, local and overseas archaeology.

19

## Abbotsbury Subtropical Gardens

**EDITOR'S PICKS** | **FOR MORE INFO, SEE P24** |

Originating around 1765, the Abbotsbury Subtropical Gardens are situated in a wooded, sheltered valley close to the popular Chesil Beach. These natural conditions create a microclimate where rare plant species, particularly unusual to England can grow.

20

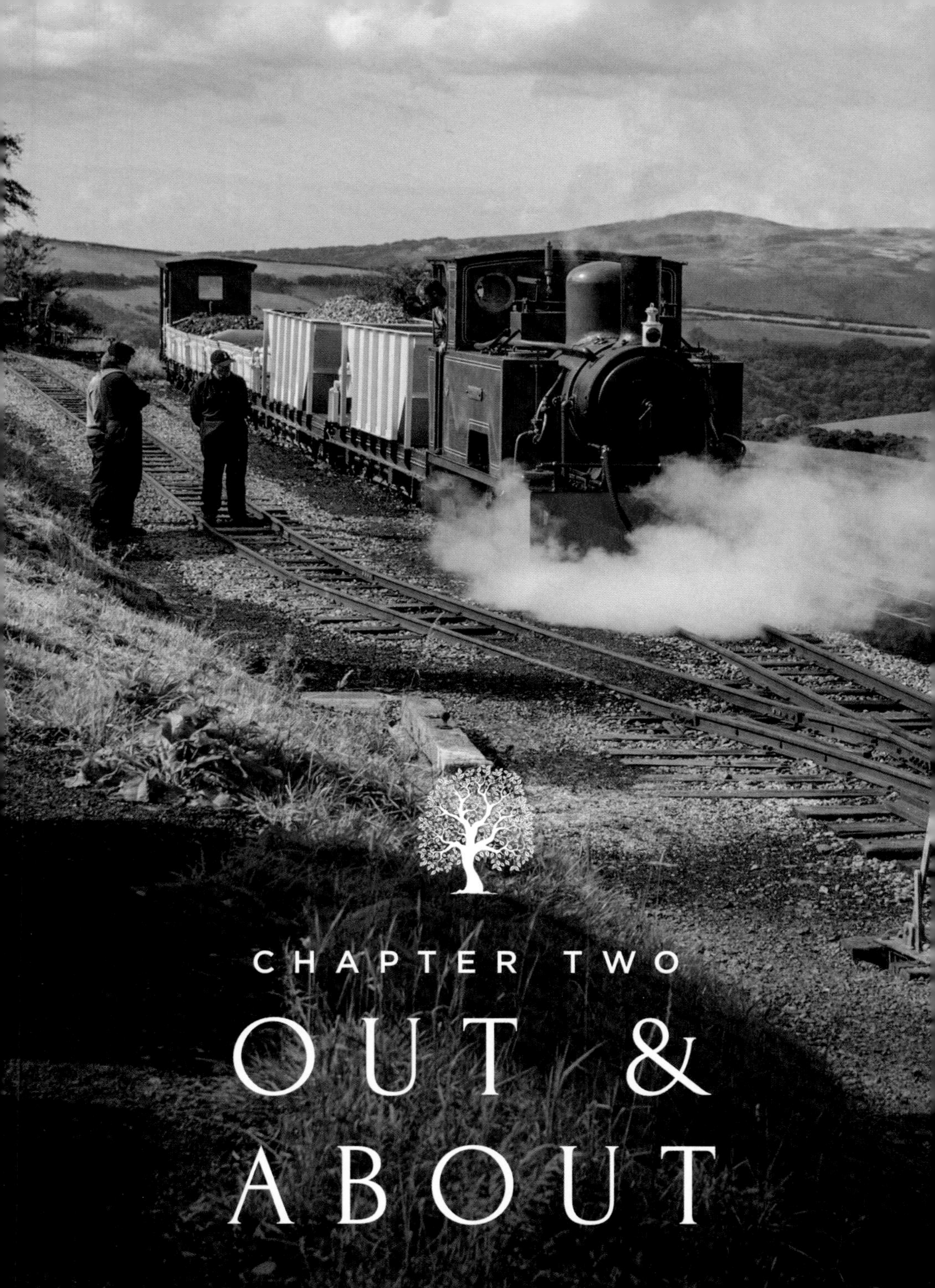

CHAPTER TWO

# OUT & ABOUT

# Ilfracombe

**OUT & ABOUT | ILFRACOMBE | EX34 9BZ**

This North Devon town has rejuvenated its image as an English seaside destination and home to the award-winning Landmark Theatre and Tunnels beaches. The scenic National Cycle Network Route to Woolacombe and The South West Coast Path from Minehead to Poole, pass through Ilfracombe.

Traditional fish and chip restaurants and seaside souvenir shops give the quintessential air of an English seaside town. However with the increased interest in surfing the Devonshire coast and the opening of restaurants including Damien Hirst's hip hangout, The Quay, Ilfracombe is becoming more attractive to a younger crowd.

## ADDRESS

Promenade

EX34 9EQ

## PHONE

01271 863001

## NEAR HERE

Lynmouth Cliff Railway (p38)

Stoned (p82)

The Stores (p117)

# Salcombe

**OUT & ABOUT | SALCOMBE | TQ8 8DE**

Salcombe is one of Devon's most picturesque harbour towns, with views over the crystal clear water. Dolphins and a multitude of fishing boats call this scenic location home. Houses in an array of pastel tones form the backdrop, which sits close to the mouth of the sparkling Salcombe-Kingsbridge Estuary.

Rolling, lush green hills frame the sheltered golden sandy coves which can be explored by boat. Devon's finest seafood and local produce are found in Salcombe's best cafés and ambient restaurants. With many offering breathtaking views, the offer is diverse, from sleek brasseries to waterside terraces.

**ADDRESS**

Market Street
TQ8 8DE

**PHONE**

01548 843927

**NEAR HERE**

South Sands Beach (p29)
The Ferry Inn (p50)
Beachhouse (p66)

# Durdle Door

**OUT & ABOUT | WEST LULWORTH | BH20 5PU**

The magnificent geological wonder, Durdle Door is a limestone arch along the Jurassic Coast rising out of the aquamarine water at 200ft high. Within the World Heritage Site, the arch is also part of the Lulworth Estate and a short walk from Lulworth Cove.

A sweeping expanse of secluded cove leads to Durdle Door, which is perfect for picnicking and relaxation. In the Summer months the inviting water attracts swimmers and snorkelers, surrounded by the awe-inspiring scenery. Just be aware there may be no lifeguard on this beach.

### ADDRESS

Durdle Door
BH20 5PU

### PHONE

01305 224132

### NEAR HERE

Lulworth Cove (p43)
Cove Fish (p142)
Corfe Castle (p168)

# Beer Beach

**OUT & ABOUT | BEER | EX12 3BZ**

Situated in the picture postcade fishing village of Beer, this sweeping shingle beach is enveloped by vertiginous limestone cliffs. Believed to have once been a preferred location for smugglers, fisherman today regularly launch their boats from the shore.

The area is famous for its mackerel and fisherman can be watched bringing in their daily catch from this Jurassic Coast beach. Coastal walks are popular in this region with far reaching views over the water being part of their appeal and reputation. Beer is on the edge of The South West Coast Path.

## ADDRESS

N/A

EX12 3BZ

## PHONE

N/A

## NEAR HERE

The Harbour Inn (p47)

Sidmouth (p19)

Lyme Regis Brewery (p141)

# Start Point Lighthouse

**OUT & ABOUT | KINGSBRIDGE | TQ7 2ET**

Erected on the most southerly headland in the county, Start Point's jagged and rocky surroundings and strong, hazardous waters led to countless shipping disasters, wrecks and loss of life until the lighthouse first shone its warning light in 1836.

Open to the public and with guided tours at specific times of the year, Start Point overlooks the busiest shipping lanes in the world. The rugged coastline surrounding the lighthouse offers scenic walks with far reaching panoramic views.

**ADDRESS**

N/A

TQ7 2ET

**PHONE**

01803 771802

**NEAR HERE**

Sea Breeze (p72)

Stokeley (p139)

@ The Bakery (p146)

# Powderham Castle

**OUT & ABOUT | EXETER | EX6 8JQ**

Built in the 14th Century by Sir Philip Courtenay, Powderham Castle is home to the Earl and Countess of Devon and their children. Bearing the Courtenay name, of French origin, the family has over one thousand years of traceable history, predominantly situated in Devon.

Powderham comes from the Dutch word Polder, meaning "the hamlet of the reclaimed marshland." The original building was the manor house and the architectural impression of a 'castle' would have been added around the 17th century. The castle and gardens can be visited throughout the year and the castle hosts various events from music to food festivals.

**ADDRESS**

Church Road
EX6 8JQ

**PHONE**

01626 890243

**NEAR HERE**

The Country Store (p136)
The Salutation Inn (p64)
Quay Antique Centre (p132)

DOUBLE LOCKS
HOTEL
DOG BOWL
Please keep wet dogs out if possible
Please use our towels
HEATED MARQUEE AREA
IN OUR GARDEN

Hot
Drinks
TAKE AWAY
TELEPHONE
TELEPHONE
DOG BOWL

# River Exe

**OUT & ABOUT | EXETER | N/A**

Travelling almost fifty miles from the Bristol Channel in the North to the English Channel in the South at Exmouth, the River Exe has played an important role in industry and trade since the Romans created a stronghold in Exeter around 50AD.

The Exe estuary is regarded as a site of special scientific interest and a significant habitat for migrating and wading birds. Scenic boat trips from Exmouth can be taken to view the diverse wildlife, which has been known to include feeding seals.

## ADDRESS

Exeter

N/A

## PHONE

N/A

## NEAR HERE

Sidmouth (p19)

Artigiano Exeter (p114)

Exeter Cathedral (p164)

# Sidmouth

**OUT & ABOUT | SIDMOUTH | EX10 8XR**

Sidmouth was a busy port in the Middle Ages and then became a fashionable holiday destination when the young future Queen Victoria visited with her parents in 1819. With beautiful gardens and many of the original Regency buildings still lining the streets, Sidmouth exudes a timeless charm.

Today, the beautiful sand and shingle beach creates perfect rock pooling opportunities and beach activities for families. Surrounded by dramatic cliffs, the town is considered the gateway to the Jurassic Coast.

## ADDRESS

Ham Lane
EX10 8XR

## PHONE

01395 516441

## NEAR HERE

The Pea Green Boat (p68)
Beer Beach (p13)
Jack in the Green Inn (p58)

# Canonteign Falls

**OUT & ABOUT | EXETER | EX6 7RH**

Canonteign is home to some of England's most spectacular waterfalls: both the natural falls created over the centuries in this valley and the picturesque falls named after the 3rd Lady Exmouth and built under her direction in 1890. The falls provide inspiration for many photographers and painters due to their striking beauty.

Canonteign's Lady Exmouth Falls were created by local miners after they had been made redundant following the closure of the estate's silver mines. The impressive waterfalls are the highest man-made waterfalls in England, measuring 70m high.

**ADDRESS**

Lower Ashton
EX6 7RH

**PHONE**

01647 252434

**NEAR HERE**

The Clipper café (p126)
Ness Cove (p22)
Torre Abbey (p158)

# Bantham Beach

**OUT & ABOUT** | **KINGSBRIDGE** | TQ7 3AN

Bantham beach is an AONB and considered one of Devon's premier surfing beaches. The beach is renowned for both its vast, breathtaking panoramic views over Bigbury Bay and Burgh Island and its multitude of water based activities for families.

Beautiful meandering coastal footpaths are popular with walkers and its wild dunes and natural charm have appealed to surfers for years. A surf academy, situated on the beach, provides professional tuition for visitors. A popular Gastrobus brings locally sourced produce and take-away picnics at specific times of the year.

## ADDRESS

Bantham

TQ7 3AN

## PHONE

01548 560897

## NEAR HERE

Beachhouse (p66)

Hope Cove (p28)

The Crabshell Inn (p56)

# Ness Cove

**OUT & ABOUT | SHALDON | TQ14 0HP**

Ness Cove is located at the foot of the Ness Headland. This secluded, mainly shingle beach is surrounded by dramatic cliffs and is popular with locals for swimming, rock-pooling and fishing. Access to the beach is down an 'old smugglers tunnel', which is a path that cuts through the Jurassic cliffs to the sea. It is believed that the path was the access route or tunnel for the smugglers that used the beach for their contraband.

On warmer evenings locals and visitors are often seen enjoying BBQs on the beach. As Ness Cove is harder to get to, it is often less busy than neighbouring beaches but facilities are limited.

## ADDRESS

SW Coast Path
TQ14 0HP

## PHONE

N/A

## NEAR HERE

Café ODE (p121)
The Clipper café (p126)
Canonteign Falls (p20)

# Shaldon Beach

**OUT & ABOUT** | **SHALDON** | TQ14 0DL

Located at the mouth of the River Teign, Shaldon Beach is particularly popular with water enthusiasts. From rowing and sailing to canoeing and fishing, this beach is a hive of activity. Large container ships can be seen navigating the narrow estuary mouth at high tide as they enter Teignmouth harbour.

Shaldon beach has a fusion of red toned sand and shingle which meets the calm waters of the estuary. Small boats are often seen bobbing about close to the beach. The Shaldon Regatta, considered one of the oldest in the country, takes place in August.

## ADDRESS

Shaldon beach

TQ14 0DL

## PHONE

N/A

## NEAR HERE

Ness Cove (p22)

Torre Abbey (p158)

Riverford Field Kitchen (p74)

# Abbotsbury Subtropical Gardens

**OUT & ABOUT | WEYMOUTH | DT3 4LA**

Originating around 1765, the Abbotsbury Subtropical Gardens are situated in a wooded, sheltered valley close to the popular Chesil Beach. These natural conditions create a microclimate where rare plant species, particularly unusual to England, can grow.

The popular celebrity gardener Alan Titchmarsh described Abbotsbury Subtropical Gardens as "one of the finest gardens I've ever visited" and it is regularly featured on the leading televised gardening shows. The gardens regularly host events, from a pop-up restaurant for a fine dining experience to nights where the gardens are beautifully illuminated.

**ADDRESS**

Buller's Way

DT3 4LA

**PHONE**

01305 871387

**NEAR HERE**

Crab House café (93)

The Hive Beach café (p112)

The Seaside Boarding House (p67)

# Blackpool Sands

**OUT & ABOUT** | **DARTMOUTH** | TQ6 0RG

Situated in a sheltered bay enveloped with evergreens and pines, is the Blue Flag awarded Blackpool Sands, in an Area of Outstanding Natural Beauty. The beach is renowned for its sparkling, crystal clear water and it is often commented that the beach looks more Mediterranean or Aegean in appearance.

On this sweeping crescent shaped beach, sand pits and water activities from kayaks to paddle boards are available for hire. You often see sailing boats dropping anchor to enjoy this unspoilt environment. Beach facilities are good for families and the beach café serves local produce and sustainably sourced seafood.

## ADDRESS

Blackpool
TQ6 0RG

## PHONE

01803 771800

## NEAR HERE

The Venus café (p106)
Radius 7 (p73)
Dartmouth Castle (p160)

# Hope Cove

**OUT & ABOUT | HOPE COVE | TQ7 3HJ**

Hope Cove is situated in South Devon's AONB and is a small seaside village close to Salcombe. With two beautiful beaches sheltered by the headland of Bolt Tail, in the curve of Bigbury Bay, the village is famous for its crab and lobster.

Along with its charming thatched cottages and clean sandy beaches, the area is also known for its unique flora and fauna and surrounding miles of rugged Heritage Coastline, including the nature reserve of Slapton Ley.

## ADDRESS

The Cottage Hotel
TQ7 3HJ

## PHONE

01548 561555

## NEAR HERE

Hope & Anchor (p55)
Bantham Beach (p21)
Salcombe (p11)

# South Sands Beach

**OUT & ABOUT** | **SALCOMBE** | **TQ8 8LE**

South Sands beach is considered one of Devon's most unspoilt beaches. It's located in an Area of Outstanding Natural Beauty at the mouth of the estuary in the pretty and affluent town of Salcombe.

Canoeing, wind surfing, catamaran sailing and even scuba diving to explore the local shipwrecks are all available from the beach. South Sands Beach is part of a cove and sheltered from the strong winds, providing a perfect sun-trap. A three mile circular walk to Bolt Head on the South West Coast Path reveals some of the most beautiful panoramic views the region has to offer.

## ADDRESS

Bolt Head
TQ8 8LE

## PHONE

N/A

## NEAR HERE

South Sands Restaurant (p84)
The Winking Prawn (p85)
Harbour Hotel & Spa (p86)

# Brixham Harbour

**OUT & ABOUT | BRIXHAM | TQ5 9BW**

Colourful houses cascade down to Brixham, one of the prettiest harbours along the Devonshire coast. A fusion of historic fishing port and contemporary industry, the harbour is home to a fleet of over 100 fishing boats and heritage trawlers, lovingly restored by passionate enthusiasts.

The local fish market on the quayside is regionally renowned and a visitor viewing platform is strategically placed so visitors can watch the busy activities of the fishing fleet. Chartered voyages are offered on some of the heritage trawlers for visitors.


## ADDRESS

Brixham, New Fish Quay
TQ5 9BW

## PHONE

01803 851854


## NEAR HERE


Breakwater Coffee Shop & Bistro (p69)

Port Espresso (p116)

The Golden Hind (p161)

# Lynton and Barnstaple Railway

**OUT & ABOUT | PARRACOMBE | EX31 4RA**

Lynton & Barnstaple Railway opened in 1898 and closed in September 1935 and was one of the world's most famous and picturesque narrow gauge railways. A two mile round trip through the dramatic and spectacular countryside of North Devon starts at Woody Bay Station, where you board an original steam engine.

The station is geared up for the family with plenty of space for picnics and an array of vintage tractors for sunny days. A station tea room with a real coal fire during the colder months offers home-baked scones and warming bowls of soup all made from locally sourced ingredients and local producers.

**ADDRESS**

Martinhoe Cross
EX31 4RA

**PHONE**

01598 763487

**NEAR HERE**

Lynmouth Cliff Railway (p38)
Annie and the Flint (p115)
Ilfracombe (p10)

# Saunton Sands

**OUT & ABOUT | SAUNTON | EX33 1LQ**

Saunton Sands in North Devon is a favourite for longboard surfers, walkers and nature enthusiasts. The beach sits in front of Braunton Burrows, one of the largest sand dune systems in Britain and recognised as a UNESCO Biosphere Reserve.

The three and a half miles of golden sand beaches have made regular appearances on camera having been the location of Robbie Williams song “Angels” and for the Olly Murs song “Hand on Heart”. Beware of strong currents to the south of the beach if you plan on taking a dip as there is no lifeguard service.

## ADDRESS

Saunton
EX33 1LQ

## PHONE

01271 890771

## NEAR HERE

The Stores (p117)
Stoned (p82)
Croyde Beach (p33)

# Croyde

**OUT & ABOUT** | **CROYDE** | EX33 1FF

Croyde lies on the South West Coast Path near to Baggy Point and is within the North Devon Coast Area of Outstanding Natural Beauty. Croyde has become popular as a surf destination and, when the conditions are right, attracts surfers from all around the world.

The wide, golden sandy beach sits between two headlands so offers some protection from the wind and sand dunes to the rear offer a natural playground for the little ones to burn off some energy. Be aware of the rip currents which can be very strong at either end of the beach and at low tide.

## ADDRESS

Croyde Road, Braunton
EX33 1FF

## PHONE

01271 890890

## NEAR HERE

Stoned (p82)
The Stores (p117)
Putsborough Beach (p39)

# Dartmouth

**OUT & ABOUT** | **DARTMOUTH** | TQ6 9YY

Dartmouth is set on the western bank of the estuary of the River Dart, which is a long narrow tidal river that runs inland as far as Totnes. Historic streets sit alongside the scenic river bank and combine to make this one of Devon's most attractive towns.

Historically, Dartmouth has been a strategic port for the Royal Navy with The Britannia Royal Naval College located on the hill overlooking the town. Be sure to soak up some of the heritage with a boat trip to Dartmouth Castle and Bayards Cove Fort. Blackpool Sands is also just a short drive from Dartmouth and is not to be missed.

## ADDRESS

Mayor's Avenue

TQ6 9YY

## PHONE

01803 834224

## NEAR HERE

Rockfish (p65)

Kingswear (p35)

Dartmouth Castle (p160)

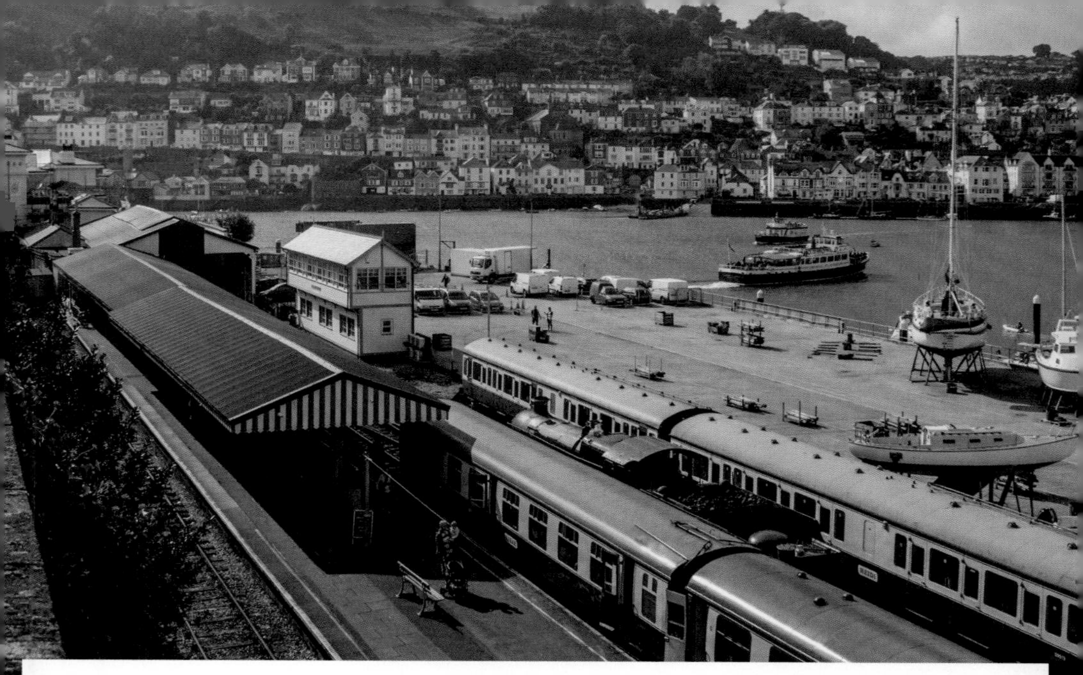

# Kingswear

**OUT & ABOUT | KINGSWEAR | TQ6 0AA**

Kingswear is the last stop on the Dartmouth Steam railway which makes a delightful way to arrive on the east bank of the River Dart. Hop off the railway and onto the frequent passenger ferry and, a few minutes later, you are in the heart of Dartmouth.

The village itself is home to several 19th century villas and a number of brightly coloured houses that look splendid when the sun shines. This charming and attractive village provides spectacular views of the sea and up the river to Totnes and a welcome break from the hustle and bustle of across the river.

## ADDRESS

The Square
TQ6 0AA

## PHONE

N/A

## NEAR HERE

Dartmouth (p34)
Rockfish (p65)
Blackpool Sands (p25)

Do Not Enter

# Lynton & Lynmouth Cliff Railway

**OUT & ABOUT | LYNMOUTH | EX35 6EQ**

Lynton and Lynmouth are two historic towns whose economic and tourist development were being significantly hampered by the 500ft cliffs which separated them in the 19th century. Over 125 years old, this funicular solved that problem and once built became the steepest in the world.

The Cliff Railway is entirely water-powered with the two cars permanently attached to each other by hauling cables. It takes 700 gallons of water to operate the cars which weigh 20 tonnes combined when fully loaded. This unique mode of transportation makes for a very exciting way to travel.

**ADDRESS**

The Esplanade

EX35 6EQ

**PHONE**

01598 753486

**NEAR HERE**

Ilfracombe (p10)

Lynton and Barnstaple Railway (p31)

St Nicholas Chapel (p156)

# Putsborough Beach

**OUT & ABOUT | PUTSBOROUGH | EX33 1LB**

Putsborough Sands is a sweeping, golden sand beach, lapped by the Atlantic, which forms the southern section of Woolacombe Sands. Close to the Baggy Point headland which provides the beach with a little shelter, the waters are popular with surfers, particularly long boarders.

Its clean waters, impressive surroundings and limited facilities appeal to those seeking a quieter and more rustic beach experience. Rock pooling and watersports are popular activities on Putsborough Beach. Dog walking is permitted at certain times of the year.

**ADDRESS**

Vention Lane

EX33 1LB

**PHONE**

01271 890231

**NEAR HERE**

Croyde Beach (p33)

The Stores (p117)

Saunton Sands (p32)

# Bournemouth

**OUT & ABOUT | BOURNEMOUTH | BH2 5AA**

Bournemouth is a seaside resort famous for its eleven miles of sandy beaches, Victorian architecture and Grade I listed church. The main beach has been attracting beach-goers since Victorian times and still remains one of Britain's favourites. On the hottest days of summer, it can get a little too busy but there are plenty of quieter alternatives nearby.

Bournemouth also has a 300m pier that dates back to 1880. On a clear day you will be able to see the Isle of Wight in the distance. The town also has a professional football club, AFC Bournemouth, known as The Cherries.

### ADDRESS

Pier Approach

BH2 5AA

### PHONE

01202 451734

### NEAR HERE

Velo Domestique (p99)

Deli Rocks (p140)

Le Petit Prince (p151)

# Weymouth

**OUT & ABOUT | WEYMOUTH | DT4 7AN**

Weymouth is a seaside town in Dorset located at the mouth of the River Wey. The esplanade is composed of an attractive arc of terraces. Much of the architecture was constructed in the Georgian and Regency periods between 1770 and 1855 and commissioned by wealthy businessmen. In the centre of the town lies Weymouth Harbour which is an attractive area to explore and full of cafés and restaurants.

Weymouth Beach is three miles long and a few minutes walk from the town centre. It was announced as the number one beach in the UK in the TripAdvisor Travellers' Choice Awards for 2017.

**ADDRESS**

Beach
DT4 7AN

**PHONE**

01305 838511

**NEAR HERE**

Delicious (p154)
The Monkey's Fist (p96)
Northe Fort (p167)

# Swanage

**OUT & ABOUT | SWANAGE | BH19 1LB**

Swanage on the Jurassic Coast is a traditional seaside town overlooking a spectacular bay with views of the Isle of Wight. The gently shelving, golden sandy beach regularly wins the Blue Flag status. Diving, sailing and swimming are all popular recreational activities taking place from Swanage Bay.

The coastline surrounding Swanage is considered of national and international ecological and geological importance. Dinosaur remains have been found in this area leading to significant archaeological interest in the region. A wonderful pier scattered with benches allows for pretty views across the water.

**ADDRESS**

Shore Road

BH19 1LB

**PHONE**

01929 766018

**NEAR HERE**

Java Independent Coffee House (p125)

Love Cake (p127)

Corfe Castle (p168)

# Lulworth Cove

**OUT & ABOUT | LULWORTH | BH20 5RQ**

Lulworth Cove is a stunning secluded cove on the Jurassic Coast UNESCO World Heritage Site which owes its existence to the collision of continents and the birth of the Alps and is considered one of the best places in the world to study geology.

Nearby is Durdle Door, a natural limestone arch whose name is derived from the Old English 'thirl' meaning bore or drill. The arch was formed about 140 million years ago and today you can see the remains of a fossil forest at the top of the arch. Well behaved dogs are permitted in specified areas.

## ADDRESS

Main Road
BH20 5RQ

## PHONE

01929 400587

## NEAR HERE

Durdle Door (p12)
Corfe Castle (p168)
Finca (p107)

# Lyme Regis Harbour

**OUT & ABOUT | LYME REGIS | DT7 3JJ**

Lyme Regis is a coastal town in West Dorset within Lyme Bay and is nicknamed "The Pearl of Dorset." The harbour for Lyme Regis is known locally as the Cobb and has served as a refuge from the sea since 1313.

If you are a sailor then the harbour provides a launch point to some of the best sailing waters in the country and if you walk to the end of the Victoria Pier you will be rewarded with a picture postcard view of Lyme Regis and beyond. Lyme Regis is ideally positioned for the Jurassic Coast and is surrounded by beautiful coastlines. As such, the area has now been awarded World Heritage Site status.

## ADDRESS

Harbour

DT7 3JJ

## PHONE

N/A

## NEAR HERE

Lyme Regis Brewery (p141)

Ryder & Hope (p137)

The Harbour Inn (p47)

# Notes

Tried our app?

bestofengland.com/app

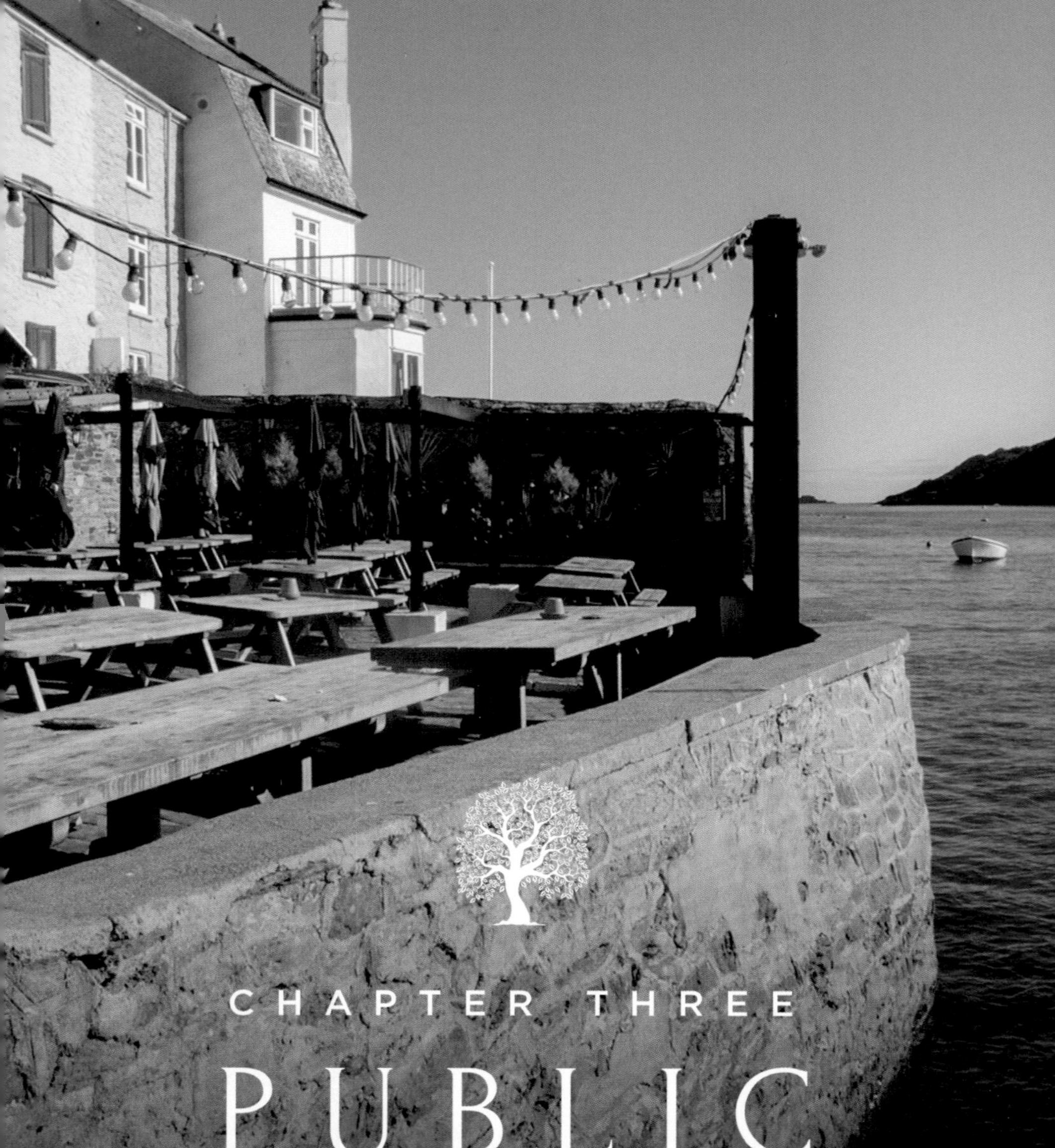

CHAPTER THREE

# PUBLIC HOUSES

# The Harbour Inn

**PUBLIC HOUSES | AXMOUTH | EX12 4AF**

The Harbour Inn is a traditional, Grade II Listed thatch roofed pub set within the quaint village of Axmouth. It is a short distance from the Axe Estuary which is popular with walkers and birdwatchers and within an Area of Outstanding Natural Beauty.

This country pub dates back to the 12th Century and retains many of the original features including a large stone fireplace and exposed wooden beams. Dishes include Lyme Bay Lobster, classic fish pie and flatbread pizzas. Well behaved children and dogs are welcome and there is a large garden to the rear.

## ADDRESS

Church Street

EX12 4AF

## PHONE

01297 20371

## NEAR HERE

Beer Beach (p13)

Sidmouth (p19)

The Bull (p94)

# Millbrook Inn

**PUBLIC HOUSES** | **KINGSBRIDGE** | TQ7 2RW

Situated in the village of South Pool in the heart of the South Hams, this idyllic spot can also be reached by boat from Salcombe when the tide is right. It is easy to reach from the local towns of Kingsbridge and Dartmouth.

Jean-Phillippe Bidart their award-winning chef, heads up the Millbrook Inn kitchen, bringing his unique, Gallic sensibility to their local and seasonal menu. Low beams, roaring fires and original stone wall features make this a popular and traditional choice.


**ADDRESS**

South Pool

TQ7 2RW

**PHONE**

01548 531581


**NEAR HERE**


Start Point Lighthouse (p14)

Sea Breeze (p72)

Stokeley (p139)

# The Ilchester Arms

**PUBLIC HOUSES** | **WEYMOUTH** | DT3 4JR

The Ilchester Arms is a family run rustic pub and restaurant in the village of Abbotsbury, serving home-made food using fresh, local produce wherever possible. Their meat, fish, vegetable and cheese suppliers are all local companies, hand-picked for their quality and seasonality.

The pub believes in keeping the menu simple and crafting dishes around what is fresh that week, alongside their classic pub favourites. The interior style is rustic with mismatched Chesterfields, farmhouse tables and shelves brimming with books and toys. The Ilchester Arms offers a family friendly environment.

## ADDRESS

9 Market Street

DT3 4JR

## PHONE

01305 873841

## NEAR HERE

Duck's Farmshop & café (p143)

Abbotsbury Subtropical Gardens (p24)

The Ilchester Arms (p49)

# The Ferry Inn

**PUBLIC HOUSES | SALCOMBE | TQ8 8ET**

The Ferry Inn is an unpretentious pub which enjoys exceptional views over the sparkling water of Salcombe harbour. On a sunny day, the terrace makes for one of the finest spots in England to enjoy a cask ale or a chilled glass of rosé.

The large modern bar and traditional rustic seating area make for a welcoming drinking hole. Enjoy Fish & Chips and West Country 8oz Rump Steak outside or indoors alongside the cosy wood burner. Conveniently located next to the ferry jetty, be sure to take some time to enjoy their seaside beer garden.

**ADDRESS**

Fore Street

TQ8 8ET

**PHONE**

01548 844000

**NEAR HERE**

The Fortescue Inn (p51)

The Wardroom (p118)

Sailor V Salcombe (p120)

# The Fortescue Inn

**PUBLIC HOUSES | SALCOMBE | TQ8 8BZ**

The Fortescue Inn in Salcombe benefits from its beautiful location tucked away and yet in the heart of Salcombe. Its whitewashed exterior and pretty hanging baskets add to the many charming original features of the pub, from its three fireplaces with wood-burners to the oak beams.

Popular with locals and visitors alike, the pub has a spacious and traditional interior with a lighter, more contemporary restaurant. Food at The Fortescue Inn is a firm favourite, with pub classics such as steak and chips as well as their stone-baked, hand-stretched pizza.

## ADDRESS

Union Street
TQ8 8BZ

## PHONE

01548 842868

## NEAR HERE

Harbour Hotel & Spa (p86)
South Sands Beach (p29)
The Ferry Inn (p50)

# The Three Horseshoes

**PUBLIC HOUSES | BURTON BRADSTOCK | DT6 4QZ**

The Three Horseshoes Pub and Kitchen is a beautiful three hundred year old thatched stone property on the Jurassic Coast in the idyllic village of Burton Bradstock. The pub is situated within walking distance of the coastal path and the scenic “Hive” beach, making it a perfect stop off en route.

The Three Horseshoes has cosy, log fires burning in the winter and a lovely suntrap of a beer garden for the summer. Chesterfield chairs in vibrant velvets and chocolate leathers, contrast with the stone floors and walls in this rustic interior. Food is kept simple and fresh, often featuring local seafood

## ADDRESS

Mill Street
DT6 4QZ

## PHONE

01308 897259

## NEAR HERE

The Seaside House (p67)
Hive Beach café (p112)
The Station Kitchen (p78)

# Hope & Anchor

**PUBLIC HOUSES | KINGSBRIDGE | TQ7 3HQ**

The Hope & Anchor pub at Hope Cove is a contemporary, coastal retreat in the peaceful and secluded seaside village of Kingsbridge, overlooking the beach. Their relaxed bed and breakfast is dog friendly too so it's ideal for all the family. With sea view decking, this is a glorious spot on a sunny day.

With impressive views and an open kitchen, the restaurant's menu has a strong focus on local produce, particularly seafood, fresh from the sea below. Their bedrooms are simple and stylish with enviable sea views, making it the perfect place to stay after exploring the local coastal paths.

## ADDRESS

Hope Cove
TQ7 3HQ

## PHONE

01548 561294

## NEAR HERE

Beach House (p66)
South Sands Beach (p29)
The Pantry (p148)

# The Crabshell Inn

**PUBLIC HOUSES | KINGSBRIDGE | TQ7 1JZ**

The Crabshell Inn is beautifully positioned on the quayside with extensive views over the water. With its south westerly aspect, the Inn basks in the sun all day. On cooler days the interior has a contemporary dining room also overlooking the water, with vast windows welcoming the view.

Aptly named, the menu at The Crabshell is picking up the pace and becoming acclaimed in the area. Featuring seafood inspired dishes and sharing platters from Brewdog beer battered fish and chips to crab goujons and crab tagliatelle, the menu is mouthwatering and the ambience buzzy.

## ADDRESS

The Quay, Embankment Road
TQ7 1JZ

## PHONE

01548 852 345

## NEAR HERE

@ The Bakery (p146)
Stokeley (p139)
Millbrook Inn (p48)

# Bankes Arms

**PUBLIC HOUSES | STUDLAND | BH19 3AU**

The Bankes Arms is an award winning pub which dates back to 1549. The pub is an old smuggler's haunt nestled in the Purbeck Hills and overlooking Studland Beach. The inn serves food all day, as well as ales from its own adjoining brewery. Prices are reasonable and portions generous.

The area around Studland is a haven for nature lovers and outdoor enthusiasts with the largest RSPB reserve located a few miles away at Arne. If you are in the area, be sure to take the cliff top path to the famous Old Harry Rocks.

## ADDRESS

Manor Road
BH19 3AU

## PHONE

01929 450225

## NEAR HERE

Shell Bay Restaurant (p89)
Rick Stein Sandbanks (p77)
Corfe Castle (p168)

# Jack in the Green Inn

**PUBLIC HOUSES | EXETER | EX5 2EE**

The Jack in the Green has recently celebrated its 25th year as a Devon dining institution. With a strict emphasis on local, quality produce, the restaurant has a reputation for its delicious cuisine and has a multitude of awards to prove it.

The pub exudes the aesthetic of a traditional pub with flagstone floors, comfortable armchairs, leather chairs and low beams. The restaurant is lighter and slightly more formal. The focus at The Jack in the Green however is the food, with contemporary twists on the classics. Its popularity continues, even after 25 years.

## ADDRESS

London Road

EX5 2EE

## PHONE

01404 822240

## NEAR HERE

Quay Antique Centre (p132)

Sidmouth (p19)

Powderham Castle (p15)

# The Thatch

**PUBLIC HOUSES** | **CROYDE** | EX33 1LZ

The Thatch is a popular and bustling pub in the heart of the seaside village of Croyde. Its traditional interior welcomes locals and guests from far and wide. Their menu features pub classics with some local ingredients and their famous Nachos, alongside real ales. The pub can get very busy and often has live bands playing.

The pub, as the name suggests, has a large thatched roof and its interior features old wooden beams, stone walls and dark, traditional pub furnishings. Breakfast is also available, offering a full English (with vegetarian options) and homemade pancakes.

## ADDRESS

14 Hobb's Hill
EX33 1LZ

## PHONE

01271 890349

## NEAR HERE

The Stores (p117)
Stoned (p82)
Putsborough Beach (p39)

PH799

The

# Bearslake Inn

**PUBLIC HOUSES | LAKE | EX20 4HQ**

The Bearslake Inn in Lake Sourton is a traditional, Grade II listed thatched roof pub nestled within the beautiful North West corner of Dartmoor. Bear or be-re comes from the old Devon word meaning wooded place and Lake is the hamlet where the farm is located; so the original name may have meant the wooded place in Lake. The original building is a Devon Longhouse which provided shelter to people and animals alike. Parts of this particular one are thought to date back to the 13th Century.

Today, the pub is a welcoming, family run establishment which is well worth stopping off at for a refreshment or bite to eat.

## ADDRESS

Sourton

EX20 4HQ

## PHONE

01837 861334

## NEAR HERE


Riverford Field Kitchen (p74)

Rockets and Rascals (p119)

Canonteign Falls (p20)

CHAPTER FOUR

# PLACES TO EAT

# The Salutation Inn

**PLACES TO EAT | TOPSHAM | EX3 0HL**

The Salutation Inn is an 18th century inn and high end restaurant in the heart of the beuatiful town of Topsham near Exeter. The three storey façade stands proudly in the centre of Topsham, an ancient fishing port with riverside walkways and small historic streets.

The inn is a few minutes walk from the waterfront and at the centre of the hotel is the GlassHouse, a light and airy glazed atrium open for light lunches and cream teas while the restaurant serves a high end taster menu inspired by modern day French cuisine.

## ADDRESS

68 Fore Street

EX3 0HL

## PHONE

01392 873060

## NEAR HERE

No Guts No Glory (p131)

Royal Albert Museum (p165)

Artigiano Exeter (p114)

# Rockfish

**PLACES TO EAT | DARTMOUTH | TQ6 9BH**

Rockfish in Dartmouth is located a couple of steps away from the spectacular River Dart and has been voted "best UK fish & chip shop" several years running. The menu is a feast of freshly caught, local seafood and they have recently transformed their kitchen to create the very same menu for coeliac's and those suffering with gluten intolerance.

This Dartmouth restaurant was the first to open, and now Rockfish has extended along Devon's seafood coastline with six locations from Plymouth to Exmouth. Located by the ferry crossing is their take-away restaurant, where you can grab a scoop of chips for a quid and take your food to the waters edge and watch the boats.

## ADDRESS

8 South Embankment
TQ6 9BH

## PHONE

01803 832800

## NEAR HERE

Kingswear (p35)
Radius 7 (p73)
Blackpool Sands (p25)

# Beachhouse

**PLACES TO EAT | KINGSBRIDGE | TQ7 3JY**

The Beachhouse is uniquely situated between the two wonderful go-to destinations Salcombe and Kingsbridge and has become a destination in itself. Transformed from a classic snack-shack, the Beachhouse has become one of Britain's top seaside venues.

The restaurant overlooks the dramatic South Milton beach where rambling and boating are the main activities. On the menu are dishes such as herby Salcombe crab, lobster Caesar salad and specials such as Italian seafood stew. They are open for breakfast, lunch and dinner yet opening hours differ throughout the year.

## ADDRESS

South Milton
TQ7 3JY

## PHONE

01548 561144

## NEAR HERE

Hope & Anchor (p55)
Hope Cove (p28)
South Sands Restaurant (p84)

# The Seaside Boarding House

**PLACES TO EAT** | **BRIDPORT** | DT6 4RB

The Seaside Boarding House overlooks the sand-coloured cliffs of Hive Beach and beyond to the majestic arm of "The Chesil". This bright restaurant looks out over the ocean, with French windows opening onto a wide terrace, where diners can enjoy the flavours of the coast accompanied by a sea breeze.

The menu features scrumptious local seafood and changes frequently with the seasons. As well as a restaurant the Seaside Boarding House has a proper bar and eight luxurious bedrooms all with sea views. Build up an appetite by strolling along the coarse sands of Hive Beach or having a dip in the sea. Alternatively you can grab a crab sandwich and head down onto the shore.

## ADDRESS

Cliff Road

DT6 4RB

## PHONE

01308 897205

## NEAR HERE

The Three Horseshoes (p54)

The Hive Beach café (p112)

The Watch House café (p113)

# The Pea Green Boat

**PLACES TO EAT | SIDMOUTH | EX10 8BB**

With panoramic views overlooking the seafront at Sidmouth, The Pea Green Boat offers the ideal backdrop to your morning coffee. With an emphasis on seasonal, local and sustainable ingredients, they only source meat from within thirty miles of the restaurant.

The simple yet vibrant interior fuses soft, sea blues with contemporary colourful fittings. Stripped wooden floors and tables are minimal and the outside dining area at the front makes an excellent al fresco dining spot on warmer days. The menu is influenced naturally by the local seafood available and pizzas are also popular.

## ADDRESS

The Esplanade
EX10 8BB

## PHONE

01395 514152

## NEAR HERE

Beer Beach (p13)
The Harbour Inn (p47)
Jack in the Green Inn (p58)

# Breakwater Coffee Shop & Bistro

**PLACES TO EAT | BRIXHAM | TQ5 9AF**

Elevated above the sea and overlooking the little cove at the breakwater in Brixham, Breakwater Coffee Shop & Bistro has beautiful views across the whole of Torbay. An outside balcony provides the perfect lunching and dining experience on warm, sunny days with views over the water.

Local, sustainable, quality produce is the focus at Breakwater. Their ingredients include fish from their local fish merchant 'Brixham Seafoods,' a third generation local fishing family. Their drinks list carries artisanal brands including Bays Brewery in Torbay and Sharpham Vineyard.

**ADDRESS**

Berry Head Road
TQ5 9AF

**PHONE**

01803 856738

**NEAR HERE**

The Golden Hind (p161)
Brixham Harbour (p30)
Port Espresso (p116)

# Sea Breeze

**PLACES TO EAT | TORCROSS | TQ7 2TQ**

Seabreeze in Torcross is a beautiful tearoom overlooking the beach within a 16th century thatched roofed cottage. The interior is modern, light and airy with whitewashed walls and accents of sea blue. The counter is often brimming with mouthwatering homebaked chocolate, carrot and orange cakes.

Miles of golden beach stretch in front of Seabreeze and the dramatic hills of Devon surround it. The café also offers breakfast pastries with lunches ranging from homemade soups to crab sandwiches. One of the favourite choices for regulars is their warm homemade scones with clotted cream.

**ADDRESS**

Slapton Sands
TQ7 2TQ

**PHONE**

01548 580697

**NEAR HERE**

Stokeley (p139)
Blackpool Sands (p25)
The Venus café (p106)

# Radius 7

**PLACES TO EAT | DARTMOUTH | TQ6 0NR**

Radius 7 is situated in the heart of Stoke Fleming village and offers beautiful sea view dining. Styled with chic, rustic interiors using reclaimed timber and beautiful hand strung Edison lighting, this restaurant is a contemporary option with a relaxed atmosphere.

Using fresh, local, seasonal produce, Radius 7 cook their entire menu to order, meaning that their dishes can be adapted to most dietary requirements. Their specials change daily, in line with the seasons and feature Devon's best produce and regular focus on the region's celebrated seafood.

## ADDRESS

New Road
TQ6 0NR

## PHONE

01803 770007

## NEAR HERE

Dartmouth (p34)
The The Venus café (p106)
Dartmouth Castle (p160)

# Riverford Field Kitchen

**PLACES TO EAT | BUCKFASTLEIGH | TQ11 0JU**

Riverford Field Kitchen is surrounded by acres of organic fruit and veg and a busy working farm. An open barn blends into the countryside, filled with long tables and a mass of colour on the walls from drying flowers.

What better place to eat than the farm where the produce is grown. All of the food served is in one sitting for both lunch and dinner, which creates a bustling atmosphere that becomes almost celebratory as the food arrives. Three courses are served at each sitting and the menu showcases the vegetables grown on-site. Riverford Field Kitchen is splendid for a special occasion or for a unique meal.

## ADDRESS

Wash Farm Bungalow

TQ11 0JU

## PHONE

01803 762074

## NEAR HERE

Timehouse Muzeum (p159)

nkuku Lifestyle Store (p130)

Torre Abbey (p158)

# The Grosvenor Arms

**PLACES TO EAT | SHAFTESBURY | SP7 8JA**

The Grosvenor Arms has been an inn since Medieval times. The original timber framed building was a busy coaching inn, originally The Red Lion and later bought by the Grosvenor family in 1820. The Grosvenor Arms today is newly refurbished whilst retaining its historical charm.

The relaxed restaurant prides itself on serving the finest ingredients and whenever possible, seasonal, local, wild and organic. The recent renovation has given The Grosvenor Arms a contemporary makeover with earthy colour tones, leather furnishings and pops of colour on Chesterfields and bar stools. The ambience is buzzy and laid back.

### ADDRESS

The Commons
SP7 8JA

### PHONE

01747 850580

### NEAR HERE

Yellow Bicycle café (p128)
The Thirsty Bird (p104)
The Tickled Pig (p76)

# The Tickled Pig

**PLACES TO EAT | WIMBORNE | BH21 1NF**

The Tickled Pig prides itself on going to extraordinary lengths to ensure that every element of their menu has been grown or reared by themselves or sourced from local Dorset suppliers who they feel share their ideals. There is a seasonal emphasis in order to showcase the diverse and delicious produce the region has to offer.

Almost all of the salads, herbs and vegetables come from the Tickled Pig's own kitchen garden, grown using organic methods. With deep inky blue walls, an open fire place, stripped wooden floors and twinkling fairy lights, the cosy interior is a wonderful partner to the considered menu.

**ADDRESS**

26 West Borough
BH21 1NF

**PHONE**

01202 886778

**NEAR HERE**

Wimbourne Minster and Chained Library (p157)
Le Petit Prince (p151)
The Thirsty Bird (p104)

# Rick Stein Sandbanks

**PLACES TO EAT | POOLE | BH13 7QB**

Vast glass windows frame the vista of the far stretching views over Poole Harbour at Rick Stein's Sandbanks restaurant. Offering classic seafood dishes infused with the subtlety of fragrant exoticism, the restaurant interior is simple with a partially open kitchen and stripped Scandinavian wood furnishings.

Porthilly Oysters from Rock and the Indonesian Seafood Curry are popular dishes with classic Fish and Chips and Crab Salad often available. This is a relaxed dining experience and of the high standard you expect of Rick Stein's establishments, it is the view that really sets it apart.

## ADDRESS

10-14 Banks Road
BH13 7QB

## PHONE

01202 283000

## NEAR HERE

Shell Bay Restaurant (p89)
Bankes Arms (p57)
Swanage (p42)

# The Station Kitchen

**PLACES TO EAT | BRIDPORT | DT6 4EW**

Situated on the edge of the Old West Bay Station platform, The Station Kitchen showcases the best of Dorset's produce from its fresh catch, succulent local meat and garden grown vegetables, cleverly fusing old world charm with contemporary culinary excellence.

The restaurant skillfully mixes luxury and rusticity through its approach to both its food and styling. The ambience, wood clad interior, soft lighting, kitsch vintage features, fresh wild flowers and soft furnishings create a cosy environment alongside the superb food. The menu changes seasonally.

## ADDRESS

Station Road
DT6 4EW

## PHONE

01308 422845

## NEAR HERE

The Watch House café (p113)
Framptons (p149)
The Three Horseshoes (p54)

# Old Market House

**PLACES TO EAT | BRIXHAM | TQ5 8AW**

The Old Market House in Brixham is a development of the old fish market building on the harbour front. Previously used as net storage for the local fishermen, the space now houses a modern restaurant with a large terrace for al fresco dining while a wood burner keeps the inside cosy in winter.

The menu is largely determined by which fish can be caught locally that season and includes local favourites such as Brixham mussels and Brixham Beer Battered Market Fish. If the sun is shining, be sure to take some time to soak up the views from the harbour side balcony.

**ADDRESS**

The Quay
TQ5 8AW

**PHONE**

01803 856891

**NEAR HERE**

The Golden Hind (p161)

Brixham Harbour (p30)

Breakwater Coffee Shop & Bistro (p69)

# Stoned

**PLACES TO EAT** | **BRAUNTON** | EX33 2JL

Stoned pizza house is the original entrepreneurial concept from a young 16 year old who set out in 2013 touring campsites and pop-ups with a wood-fired pizza oven in tow. They specialise in stone baked foods, which have become a huge hit and resulted in this popular restaurant in Braunton.

As well as being renowned for great pizza, you can rock up to the restaurant in the morning for pastries, freshly baked goods and yesterdays left-over bread toasted with jam, free with any coffee or hot drink. Throughout the summer months they still run the pop-up pizza ovens too.

## ADDRESS

Exeter Road
EX33 2JL

## PHONE

01271 817999

## NEAR HERE

Putsborough Beach (p39)
Croyde (p33)
The Stores (p117)

# The Quay

**PLACES TO EAT | ILFRACOMBE | EX34 9EQ**

The Quay restaurant is situated in the picturesque North Devon coastal town of Ilfracombe and offers mesmerising views of the sea and harbour from its bar, Harbourside and Atlantic rooms. French doors lead to seascapes which have inspired some of The Quay's seashell paintings.

The restaurant is famous for its original art works by one of this generation's most celebrated artists, Damien Hirst, who owns The Quay. It is also renowned for its fresh, locally sourced produce, with an emphasis on seafood. Dishes are simply presented from a menu that takes inspiration from classic British and European cuisine.

## ADDRESS

11 The Quay
EX34 9EQ

## PHONE

01271 868090

## NEAR HERE

St Nicholas Chapel (p156)
Annie and the Flint (p115)
Saunton Sands (p32)

# South Sands Restaurant

**PLACES TO EAT | SALCOMBE | TQ8 8LL**

South Sands Restaurant presents some of the most sensational views in Devon, with panoramic outlooks over the estuary. Its elevated position and proximity to the beach, give the impression of actually being on the water. This New England style restaurant with its muted colours, bare wood and wide terrace for al fresco dining, is considered one of the best seafood restaurants in Salcombe.

South Sands Restaurant specialises in seafood and uses the freshest ingredients, sourced locally where possible. The sunny terrace is popular during the Summer months and the whole restaurant has a vibrant ambience.

## ADDRESS

Bolt Head
TQ8 8LL

## PHONE

01548 845900

## NEAR HERE

The Winking Prawn (p85)

Beachhouse (p66)

The Ferry Inn (p50)

# The Winking Prawn

**PLACES TO EAT | SALCOMBE | TQ8 8LD**

The Winking Prawn restaurant is reminiscent of a large sunlit beach hut. Perched on the waters edge at North Sands in Salcombe, this shabby chic café is strewn with colourful bunting and fresh flowers on the tables. Serving English breakfasts, fresh fish lunches, buckets of prawns and even summer BBQs, the Winking Prawn has been popular for twenty years.

The Winking Prawn's huge sun deck facing the sea is a perfect spot during the warmer Summer months or even for a hot chocolate in the cool of the Winter. The beach is a huge attraction and the Salcombe Dairy Ice Cream van is a resident in the summer too.

## ADDRESS

North Sands
TQ8 8LD

## PHONE

01548 842326

## NEAR HERE

South Sands Beach (p29)
The Wardroom (p118)
Sailor V Salcombe (p120)

# Harbour Hotel & Spa

**PLACES TO EAT | SALCOMBE | TQ8 8JH**

The award-winning Salcombe Harbour Hotel & Spa is recognised as one of the most desirable waterside hotels in the UK. This is a coastal retreat with a yacht-club style ambience. Along with an indulgent spa for relaxing, the waterside restaurant and wide outdoor terraces enjoy a celebrated panoramic vista for spectacular al fresco dining, overlooking one of the most dramatic coastlines.

The hotel's Jetty restaurant takes full advantage of its estuary location, with menus created by award winning Chef Alex Aitken, who delivers fresh and seasonal dishes. The Crustacean Bar offers the day's fresh catch.

## ADDRESS

Cliff Road
TQ8 8JH

## PHONE

01548 844444

## NEAR HERE

The Ferry Inn (p50)
The Bake House (p150)
The Fortescue Inn (p51)

# The Pig and Pallet

**PLACES TO EAT | TOPSHAM | EX3 0JB**

Pig and Pallet is a fun, energetic and passionate charcuterie/ deli/eatery in Topsham. This carnivorous café is housed inside a converted barn with relaxed and informal trestle table seating and an interior partly created from wooden pallets.

Pig and Pallet offer an amazing selection of local bread, cured meats, burgers and other BBQ delights. Breakfasts and brunches are done in style with dishes including full Devon fry ups, scrambled eggs with smoked salmon and bacon mac n cheese. Dinner is an even bigger affair with pulled pork baps, ribs and cheeseburgers. Vegetarian options are available.

**ADDRESS**

10 Topsham Quay
EX3 0JB

**PHONE**

01392 668129

**NEAR HERE**

The Salutation Inn (p64)
Quay Antique Centre (p132)
Mangos café (p109)

# L'Estuaire Restaurant

**PLACES TO EAT | TOPSHAM | EX3 0JB**

"Mange bien, riez souvent, aimez beaucoup!" Eat well, laugh often, love much! This is the philosophy behind L'estuaire. This popular, contemporary restaurant serves French classics in a relaxed and friendly environment.

A stylishly modern, light, open-plan space with high ceilings, is where dishes such as baked Camembert, mussels, steak tartare and seafood platters are served to delighted diners. The bar is a great place to order a wide range of drinks including wines and spirits from around the globe.

## ADDRESS

The Quay
EX3 0JB

## PHONE

01392 876801

## NEAR HERE

The Pig and Pallet (p87)
Powderham Castle (p15)
Royal Albert Museum (p165)

# Shell Bay Seafood Restaurant

**PLACES TO EAT | STUDLAND | BH19 3BA**

With expansive floor to ceiling windows and a spectacular outdoor terrace area showcasing the unrivalled surrounding scenery, Shell Bay Seafood Restaurant is located on the edge of the Isle of Purbeck, overlooking Brownsea Island. Their a la carte menu is packed with fresh, local seafood and produce from the surrounding areas.

Their menu is seasonal and they are proud to source from local growers and fishermen. Sunday Times Magazine quoted Shell Bay as "An eatery with a panoramic view out to Brownsea Island that is almost as stunning as the beautiful fresh fish they serve."

## ADDRESS

Ferry Road

BH19 3BA

## PHONE

01929 450363

## NEAR HERE


Rick Stein Sandbanks (p77)

Bankes Arms (p57)

Corfe Castle (p168)

# James and White

**PLACES TO EAT | CHRISTCHURCH | BH23 1BW**

James and White in Christchurch is the place to go for indulgent breakfasts, burgers and Sunday roasts. The ingredients are locally sourced wherever possible and renowned for their presentation. The rustic yet contemporary decor provides a calming place to enjoy their menu which focuses on seafood and grills.

Tranquil greys and blues are mixed with white brick tiles and natural textures such as crate shelving, wood panel counters and exposed light fixtures. James and White keep evenings interesting, with burger Mondays, steak and wine nights and acoustic music events taking place throughout the week.

## ADDRESS

17 Church Street

BH23 1BW

## PHONE

01202 485485

## NEAR HERE

Christchurch Priory Church (p166)

Coffee & Dice (p102)

Deli Rocks (p140)

# Crab House Café

**PLACES TO EAT | WEYMOUTH | DT4 9YU**

The Crab House Café is a delightful rustic seaside hut with a vista of the shingled Chesil Beach on the opposite side of the inlet. The interior is joyfully nautical, the fish sustainable and the prices fair.

Expect delicacies such as Skate Wing roasted with chorizo, paprika and spring onion and Monk tail fillet poached with garlic and rosemary oil. We recommend ordering the Portland oysters as they have travelled but 30 feet from sea to your plate having been collected from the restaurant's own oyster beds which can be seen from the restaurant.

**ADDRESS**

Ferrymans Way
DT4 9YU

**PHONE**

01305 788867

**NEAR HERE**

The Monkey's Fist (p96)
Weymouth (p41)
Abbotsbury Subtropical Gerdens (p24)

# The Bull

**PLACES TO EAT** | **BRIDPORT** | **DT6 3LF**

The Bull is a relaxed, award-winning boutique hotel in the market town of Bridport, surrounded by the West Dorset hills and stunning coastline. With a menu focusing on local seafood and delicious regional produce, their candlelit restaurant and rustic approach will make you want to stay for a few nights and indulge in luxury and fine cuisine.

Unwind in front of a crackling open log fire with a glass of wine on colder days or in their pretty courtyard garden, twinkling with fairy lights on Summer evenings with a cocktail from their Venner cocktail bar. Their rooms are luxurious with crisp white linens and some rooms feature vintage roll top baths, excellent after a day walking along the windswept coast.

## ADDRESS

34 East Street

DT6 3LF

## PHONE

01308 422878

## NEAR HERE


Framptons (p149)

The Station Kitchen (p78)

The Watch House café (p113)

# Il Porto

**PLACES TO EAT** | **WEYMOUTH** | **DT4 8TR**

Il Porto is a traditional Italian restaurant in Weymouth situated within an historical building off of Weymouth's picturesque harbour. Large elevated windows make for an ideal spot to people watch in bustling Hope Square which is overlooked by the restaurant.

The restaurant is housed within the converted brewery which had been brewing beer since 1252 being ideally located next to the fresh water spring at Chapelhay and not far from the barley fields of Radipole. This authentic Italian restaurant was founded by two brothers with a passion for great food and the Mediterranean sense of community.

## ADDRESS

Hope Square
DT4 8TR

## PHONE

01305 457870

## NEAR HERE

Delicious (p154)
Northe Fort (p167)
Weymouth (p41)

# The Monkey's Fist

**PLACES TO EAT | WEYMOUTH | DT4 8TR**

The Monkey's Fist is an open plan bistro with a simple, urban interior of glass topped wooden tables, stone flooring and pendant lights. It showcases the outstanding food created by Italian chef Francesco Pecchi and the menu takes inspiration from its proximity to the sea. Dishes include pan fried scallops, crab linguine and seafood risotto.

Situated on the bustling Hope Square in the heart of Weymouth, The Monkey's Fist aims to create delicious high-quality Italian dishes while championing Dorset ingredients and local producers. Be sure to stop by on Wednesday evenings for their seven course taster menu.

**ADDRESS**

2 Hope Square
DT4 8TR

**PHONE**

01305 457446

**NEAR HERE**

Il Porto (p95)
Weymouth (p41)
Crab House café (93)

# Notes

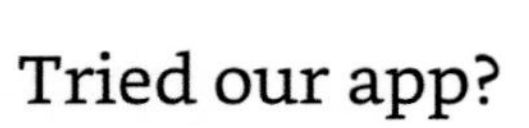


bestofengland.com/app

CHAPTER SIX

# CAFÉS

# Velo Domestique

**CAFÉS & TEA ROOMS | BOURNEMOUTH | BH5 2JB**

Other than the expansive beach, Seabourne Road is one of the best places to visit when in Bournemouth. Head to Velo Domestique and get your bike fixed and your fix of locally roasted coffee from Whipskid. They offer same day bike services as well as bespoke builds for those after a unique ride.

The café sells an interesting choice of light bites including souvlaki flatbread, chilli bean bowl and canibal pancakes. You can also purchase unique cycle clothing and your regular accessories from the shop and a new bike if you want. Even if bikes aren't your thing, the café and shop are worth a stop.

**ADDRESS**

176-180 Seabourne Road
BH5 2JB

**PHONE**

01202 432265

**NEAR HERE**

Coffee & Dice (p102)
Deli Rocks (p140)
James and White (p92)

HONDA

# Coffee & Dice

**CAFÉS & TEA ROOMS | BOURNEMOUTH | BH7 6DE**

Coffee and Dice is a new concept which has taken Bournemouth by surprise. Between 10am and 11pm daily, you can enjoy a choice of over 500 games to play, while enjoying your favourite hot beverage. There is a small entrance fee of £4, but if the weather is bad and you have plenty of time on your hands, then this is a fantastic option.

They serve a small selection of light bites and sharing boards and if you're worried that you'll have nobody to play with if visiting alone, then look out for a sign on another table welcoming you to join in the fun. Re-visit your childhood and while away a few hours.

## ADDRESS

778 Christchurch Road

BH7 6DE

## PHONE

01202 309938

## NEAR HERE

Velo Domestique (p99)

Christchurch Priory (p166)

Bournemouth (p40)

# Bermuda

**CAFÉS & TEA ROOMS** | **BOURNEMOUTH** | **BH2 5PW**

Bermuda is a seaside café with a tropical twist. This establishment serves guests with a plethora of mediterranean cuisine alongside their nourishing organic Juice Bar. Sandwiches are made using freshly baked bread and you can choose your combination, from Stonebaked and Sourdough to Gluten Free.

Wall to wall wood cladding makes for an intimate and rustic interior where guests can come and enjoy dishes such as falafel burgers, Bermuda style fishcakes and Greek salad. Bermuda café aims to provide at a fair price, nutritious, well-prepared meals, using international and British ingredients.

## ADDRESS

23 Poole Hill
BH2 5PW

## PHONE

01202 557041

## NEAR HERE

Le Petit Prince (p151)
South Coast Roast (p124)
Velo Domestique (p99)

# The Thirsty Bird

**CAFÉS & TEA ROOMS | WIMBORNE | BH21 1DS**

The Thirsty Bird is a relaxed and beautifully designed café serving speciality coffee, delicious cheeses and charcuterie alongside a decent wine menu. They believe in serving quality produce, whilst creating a welcoming, friendly atmosphere where you can truly relax and take some time out.

The Thirsty Bird has a light, white interior with pops of vibrant turquoise. Twinkling, strings of light bulbs and soft grey furnishings are offset against the tropical green plants sprinkled throughout the café. Their window seats are wonderful for watching the world go by and dogs are allowed.

## ADDRESS

3 East Street

BH21 1DS

## PHONE

01202 887722

## NEAR HERE

The Tickled Pig (p76)

Wimborne Library (p157)

Finca (p107)

# The Galley Café

**CAFÉS & TEA ROOMS | LYME REGIS | DT7 3QE**

Founded by Keian Gillet, a chef with international credentials and a passionate board-rider, the Galley Café brings relaxed surf chic to Lyme Regis. Surf boards are suspended from the ceiling and walls, whilst the decor exudes an airy, seaside inspired vibe with pale blue wood cladding and white walls.

The Galley team pride themselves on the fact that almost every item on offer in the café, from the best-selling Guinness cake to the wide selection of savoury flatbreads, is made fresh on the premises. Their cooked breakfasts are gaining a popular reputation and they claim they are the best in town.

**ADDRESS**

14 Broad Street
DT7 3QE

**PHONE**

01297 445008

**NEAR HERE**

Ryder & Hope (p137)
Lyme Regis Harbour (p44)
The Harbour Inn (p47)

# Venus Café

**CAFÉS & TEA ROOMS | KINGSBRIDGE | TQ7 4AZ**

If you're looking for delicious, sustainable, locally sourced food in a wonderful beach setting, Venus Café is the place to visit. Their philosophy is reinforced in their strapline 'Loving the Beach,' and this ethos ensures that their customers' needs are balanced carefully with environmental and social considerations.

Their mission is to be the greenest beach café and awards such as the Queen's Award for Enterprise in Sustainable Development in 2005 and 2010 acknowledged Venus café as 'a rare example of a sustainable café chain'. Views over the water and from their glass fronted deck are exceptional.

## ADDRESS

Warren Road

TQ7 4AZ

## PHONE

01548 810141

## NEAR HERE

Blackpool Sands (p25)

Dartmouth Castle (p160)

Radius 7 (p73)

# Finca

**CAFÉS & TEA ROOMS | DORCHESTER | DT1 1QS**

Finca is an independent coffee shop serving coffee and beans roasted in-house by hand in their small batch roaster. People flood to Finca in Dorchester for its outstanding coffee. The rustic interior, parquet wood floor and exposed brick wall create a simple, relaxed ambience.

On warmer days they open their bi-fold doors, making it a great spot for people watching. Their service is renowned for being friendly and their homemade cakes and toasted sandwiches are popular.

**ADDRESS**

41 Great Western Road
DT1 1QS

**PHONE**

01305 300400

**NEAR HERE**

Durdle Door (p12)
Lulworth Cove (p43)
Weymouth (p41)

# The Boat Shed Café

**CAFÉS & TEA ROOMS | LULWORTH | BH20 5RQ**

Once a lock-up for those who made a living from the sea, The Boat Shed Café takes inspiration from both its history and surroundings, with its nautically themed interior and menu featuring many seafood dishes.

With the recently added terrace, you can dine in the perfect spot to admire the panoramic view across Lulworth Cove to the cliffs. A cup of tea, a quick snack or a light meal can be enjoyed whilst taking in the great views. Homemade cakes and coffee are also available.


**ADDRESS**

Main Road Lower

BH20 5RQ

**PHONE**

01929 400810


**NEAR HERE**


Corfe Castle (p168)

Durdle Door (p12)

Finca (p107)

# Mangos Café

**CAFÉS & TEA ROOMS** | **EXETER** | EX2 4AN

Mangos, located on Exeter Quay is a coffee house and wine bar serving contemporary food such as superfood salads and smashed avocado, alongside fine wine. The café is situated in one of the quay's original cellars, which creates an atmospheric space, with its curved ceilings and hanging filament bulbs.

Their open terrace overlooks the quayside and cobbled pavements. Using a combination of locally sourced ingredients and influences from the coffee capital of Australia, Mangos Café invite you to kick back inside their cosy lounge or enjoy the views outside, with fresh food, decent wine & friendly service.

## ADDRESS

Kings Wharf, The Quay
EX2 4AN

## PHONE

01392 499991

## NEAR HERE

Exeter Cathedral (p164)
No Guts No Glory (p131)
The Exploding Bakery (p147)

CORFE CASTLE
PRIVATE

# The Hive Beach Café

**CAFÉS & TEA ROOMS | BURTON BRADSTOCK | DT6 4RF**

With spectacular views across Lyme Bay and Chesil Beach, The Hive Beach Café in Burton Bradstock has a committed approach to sourcing local and sustainable seafood and produce with a menu that 'slowly evolves with the seasons'. The Hive recently received rave reviews from the late British food critic AA Gill.

The cakes and sweet indulgences are created by their team in their micro bakery in Burton Bradstock and are delicious served alongside a frothy latte whilst soaking up the breathtaking Jurassic Coast that surrounds you. Expect to queue for lunch but that just proves its growing popularity.

## ADDRESS

Beach Road
DT6 4RF

## PHONE

01308 897070

## NEAR HERE

The Seaside House (p67)
The Three Horseshoes (p54)
The Station Kitchen (p78)

# The Watch House Café

**CAFÉS & TEA ROOMS | BRIDPORT | DT6 4EN**

The sister restaurant to The Hive, The Watch House café is situated on the golden shingle beach of West Bay, overlooking the dramatic Jurassic Coastline with its imposing cliffs. The menu, like The Hive, is local, sustainable and ethically produced with an emphasis on seafood.

Its black wood clad exterior with large windows overlooking the sea, houses a simple interior of soft greys, black chalkboards, wood floors and a delicatessen style counter filled with their home-baked produce. Extensive outdoor seating for warmer days is perfect for enjoying the seafood taster board.

## ADDRESS

West Bay
DT6 4EN

## PHONE

01308 459330

## NEAR HERE

The Station Kitchen (p78)
The Hive Beach café (p112)
The Seaside Boarding House (p67)

# Artigiano Exeter

**CAFÉS & TEA ROOMS | EXETER | EX4 3PZ**

Artigiano is an innovative and stylish café/bar situated in Exeter. This establishment prides itself on providing a relaxing space to enjoy 'cult caffeine, juices, smoothies and feel good food by day', and 'craft beer, fine wine, cocktails and raw music with friends by night'.

Artigiano's large studio space allows for customers to sit down with a coffee and not feel rushed or overcrowded. There is a distinct industrial style that mixes fun colours and patterns with stainless steel furniture and natural textures, adding to its contemporary and stylish ambience.

## ADDRESS

248 High Street
EX4 3PZ

## PHONE

01392 499169

## NEAR HERE

The Exploding Bakery (p147)
Royal Albert Memorial Museum (p165)
No Guts No Glory (p131)

# Annie and the Flint

**CAFÉS & TEA ROOMS | ILFRACOMBE | EX34 9EY**

Exposed, whitewashed bricks, fresh flowers and soft grey paintwork create the interior style of Annie and the Flint café in Ilfracombe. Furnished with vintage travel trunks and leather armchairs, the café offers delicious cakes served with coffee and papers in a relaxed, ambient setting.

The menu includes granola with natural yoghurt, freshly prepared salads and healthy smoothies and juices. Homemade produce and local ingredients are key to the Annie and the Flint philosophy. Coffee is their speciality and Origin Coffee is their house brand, renowned for its ethical, sustainable practices.

## ADDRESS

126 High Street
EX34 9EY

## PHONE

07479 318778

## NEAR HERE

The Quay Restaurant (p83)
St Nicholas Chapel (p156)
Putsborough Beach (p39)

# Port Espresso

**CAFÉS & TEA ROOMS | BRIXHAM | TQ5 8ER**

Port Espresso began life when the two founders Karen Miller and Dan Joselin crossed paths. They both decided to put their talents in design and food together to create the ultimate coffee shop in Brixham.

Karen's design talents have seen the coffee shop grow into a stylish and vibrant space with quirky accents. 3D wallpaper, geometric cushions and acrylic ghost chairs make the space fun and dynamic. The source of the coffee is a closely guarded secret but know for sure, it tastes fantastic.

**ADDRESS**

26 Middle Street
TQ5 8ER

**PHONE**

01803 411120

**NEAR HERE**

Breakwater Coffee Shop & Bistro (p69)
The Golden Hind (p161)
Brixham Harbour (p30)

# The Stores

**CAFÉS & TEA ROOMS | CROYDE | EX33 1LF**

The Stores in Croyde is a stylish, contemporary café and popular choice with hip surfers and holiday makers. They source as much of their produce from Devon or within the South West region as possible and their breakfast and lunch menus offer numerous healthy options from smashed avocado on sourdough to homemade soup.

The interior design projects an industrial cool ambience, with bright yellow table legs and spots of colour amongst the muted greys and wood furnishings. This a popular venue for an iced-coffee and overnight apple bircher or for simply picking up a loaf of freshly baked sourdough bread.

### ADDRESS

1 St Marys Road
EX33 1LF

### PHONE

01271 890780

### NEAR HERE

Saunton Sands (p32)
Stoned (p82)
Croyde Beach (p33)

# The Wardroom

**CAFÉS & TEA ROOMS | SALCOMBE | TQ8 8BU**

With beautiful views across the estuary, The Wardroom Café is a popular place to sit and watch the buzz of Salcombe from one of their seafront tables, whilst sampling from their simple and delicious, seafood inspired menu with a glass of chilled wine.

The interior is bright and spacious at The Wardroom, and the walls are covered with illustrations, showing the various boats that frequent the harbour. Everything they sell is freshly cooked in their kitchen and locally sourced wherever possible. Seafood chowders, crab cakes and crab sandwiches often feature on the menu and are customer favourites.

**ADDRESS**

19 Fore Street
TQ8 8BU

**PHONE**

01548 843333

**NEAR HERE**

The Bake House (p150)
The Ferry Inn (p50)
Sailor V Salcombe (p120)

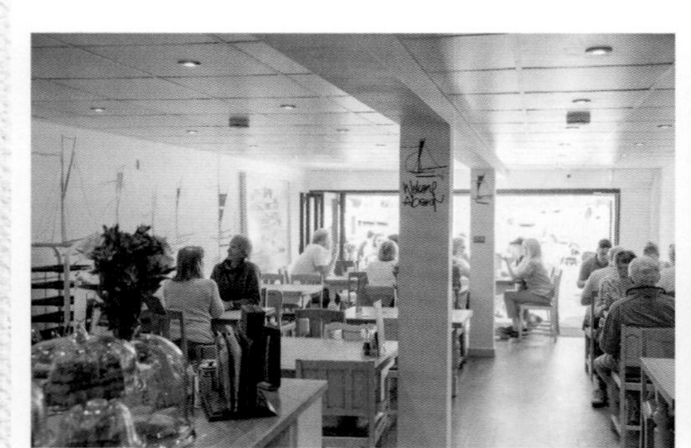

# Rockets and Rascals

**CAFÉS & TEA ROOMS** | **PLYMOUTH** | PL1 2JL

Rockets and Rascals is an outstanding venue for all things related to cycling. Opened in the spring of 2013, with a mission to get people riding bikes, they are now Plymouth's only award winning bicycle shop, and in 2014 opened their second emporium in Poole.

What makes this store unique is that it's not only a store but there's also a fantastic café attached, serving healthier breakfast options, along with cakes and great tasting coffee. At Rocket & Rascals you can browse a range of great new bikes for sale, meet knowledgeable staff, cycling enthusiasts, or simply relax with one of their delicious coffees.

## ADDRESS

7 Parade

PL1 2JL

## PHONE

01752 262170

## NEAR HERE

Bantham Beach (p21)

Bearslake Inn (p62)

Riverfield Field Kitchen (p74)

# Sailor V

**CAFÉS & TEA ROOMS | SALCOMBE | TQ8 8JF**

Sailor V is a cafe and restaurant situated at the top of the steps by the East Portlemouth Ferry in Salcombe, recently voted the best seaside resort in the UK and one of our favourites.

Formerly the old town bank, the decor of this reincarnation takes inspiration from the speakeasies of the 1920s. Hot dogs, ice cream sundaes and milkshakes are their signature dishes. Breakfasts are good value, service is quick, the staff are friendly and dogs are welcome. What's not to like?

## ADDRESS

36 Fore Street
TQ8 8JF

## PHONE

01548 843555

## NEAR HERE

Harbour Hotel & Spa (p86)
The Wardroom (p118)
South Sands Restaurant (p84)

# Café ODE

**CAFÉS & TEA ROOMS | SHALDON | TQ14 0HP**

Café Ode is renowned for its sustainable approach to using quality, ethical and seasonal ingredients in a family friendly environment. Architecturally the café was created from the original Ness stables and is considered a fusion of art renovation, conversion and new sustainable build.

Café ODE also offers take-away dishes, served by chefs in their eco conscious interior. With great views over the water, communal outside and inside seating, a grass area for kids, bike racks and even electric car charging points for customers, the café has won a multitude of awards for its sustainability and quality food.

### ADDRESS

Ness Drive
TQ14 0HP

### PHONE

01626 873427

### NEAR HERE

Ness Cove (p22)
The Clipper café (p126)
Shaldon Beach (p23)

# South Coast Roast

**CAFÉS & TEA ROOMS | BOURNEMOUTH | BH2 6EJ**

With high ceilings and an industrial aesthetic, South Coast Roast is regionally renowned for their exceptional coffee. Their grab and go approach has made this a popular choice for locals getting their morning caffeine fix alongside their delicious baked goods and sandwiches with a vegetarian/vegan focus.

Supplying coffee beans from traceable farms from Colombia to Tanzania, they can grind your coffee as you wait. Each coffee flavour is described on little chalkboards, so you can select your beans or barista made coffee with more depth and insight. Their gluten free banana cake and sourdough bread are favourites.

## ADDRESS

24 Richmond Hill
BH2 6EJ

## PHONE

01202 551197

## NEAR HERE

Bermuda (p103)
Le Petit Prince (p151)
Coffee and Dice (p102)

# Java Independent Coffee House

**CAFÉS & TEA ROOMS | SWANAGE | BH19 1DF**

Just off the beaten track and tucked away in a little courtyard is Java Independent Coffee House. This intimate cafe is a haven for those who love quality coffee, quirky interiors and vegetarian and vegan dishes.

The interior is colourful and eclectic with papier-mâché furniture and walls adorned with paintings by local artists. The lunch menu changes daily but expect dishes such as curried lentil, sweet potato and coconut soup and vegetarian shepherd's pie. There are a few tables for al fresco dining if the weather permits and it's dog friendly too.

## ADDRESS

Tilly Mead,
Commercial Road
BH19 1DF

## PHONE

N/A

## NEAR HERE

Love Cake (p127)
Corfe Castle (p168)
Bankes Arms (p57)

# The Clipper Café

**CAFÉS & TEA ROOMS | TEIGNMOUTH | TQ14 0DL**

The views from the terrace of the Clipper Cafe in Teignmouth are magnificent. Sitting right by the water's edge and overlooking the River Teign, the tables offer a great position from breakfast through to dinner.

The Clipper Cafe's resident chef Gino is passionate about sourcing the best quality local produce.  Their bread is baked fresh at the Shaldon Bakery, their seasonal vegetables are grown within one mile of the café and Gino has been known to venture out to Lyme Bay to catch the fish himself!

## ADDRESS

26 Strand

TQ14 0DL

## PHONE

01626 873747

## NEAR HERE

Ness Cove (p22)

Café ODE (p121)

Shaldon Beach (p23)

# Love Cake

**CAFÉS & TEA ROOMS | SWANAGE | BH19 2NX**

Behind the rustic stone exterior is Love Cake. This independent cafe, deli and cake emporium is simple and stylish with a homely ambience, modern country interior and fresh pastries made daily.

A great selection of drinks and coffee line the shabby chic crate shelves. There are plenty of seats for you to relax on and select a dish from the menu which is full of tempting treats from cream teas and cakes to lunch dishes including venison burgers and nachos.

## ADDRESS

42 High Street
BH19 2NX

## PHONE

01929 475664

## NEAR HERE

Java Independent Coffee House (p125)

Bankes Arms (p57)

Rick Stein Sandbanks (p77)

# Yellow Bicycle Café

**CAFÉS & TEA ROOMS | BLANDFORD FORUM | DT11 7AR**

With a bicycle inspired decor, Yellow Bicycle Cafe is a contemporary spot in the heart of Blandford Forum. Popular for its innovative menu using fresh, high quality local ingredients, their artisanal coffee and their home-baked bread is also a hit.

The interior is a fusion of white walls, wooden floors and accents of dark grey with vibrant decorative highlights of yellow bicycle parts, suspended from the walls. Magazines and books are available for customers to read as they sample dishes from their highly regarded menu.

**ADDRESS**

30a Salisbury St
DT11 7AR

**PHONE**

01258 480356

**NEAR HERE**

The Thirsty Bird (p104)
The Tickled Pig (p76)
Le Petit Prince (p151)

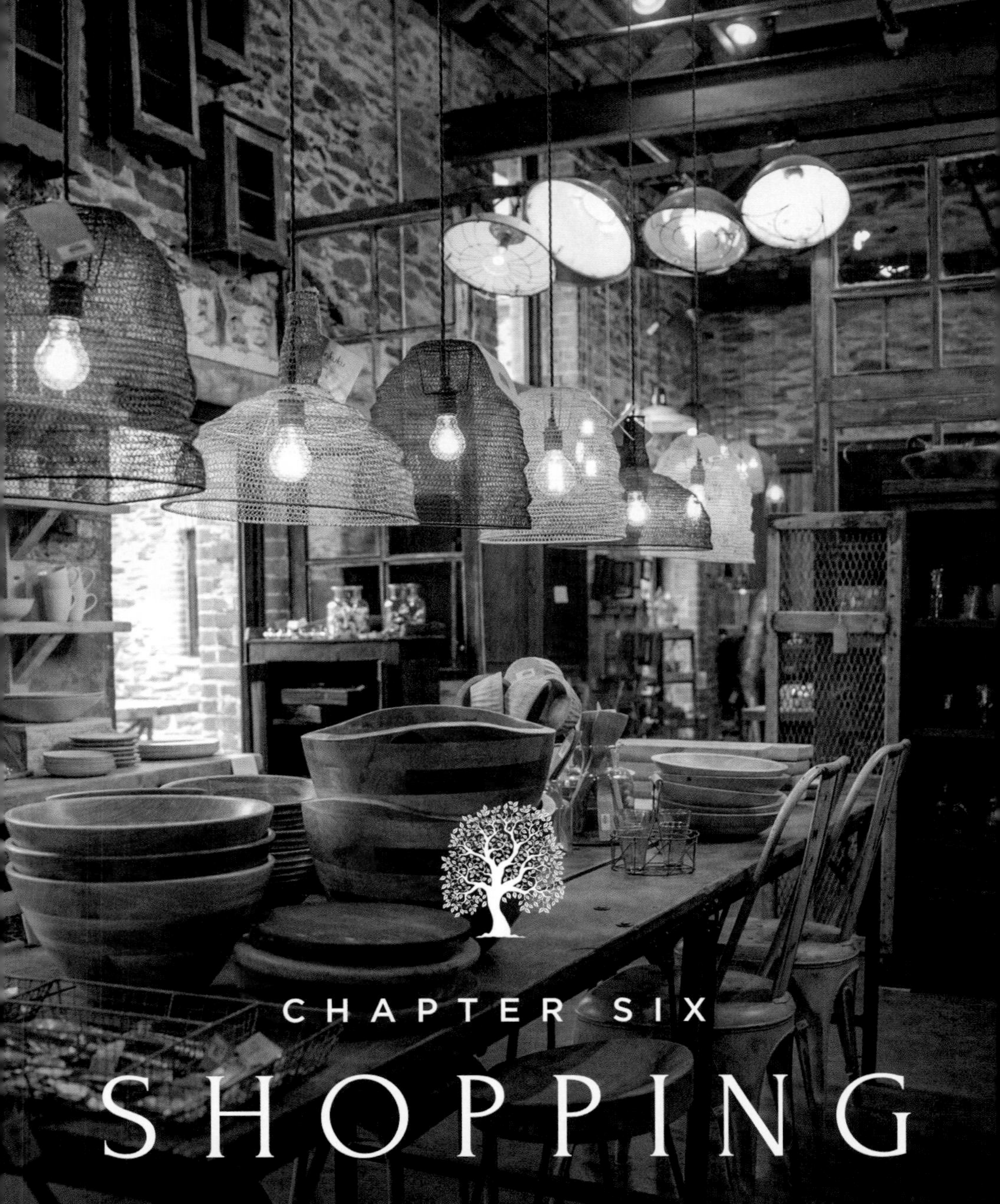

CHAPTER SIX

# SHOPPING

# nkuku lifestyle store

**SHOPPING** | **HARBERTONFORD** | **TQ9 7PS**

nkuku is one of a kind and sources some of the most attractive lifestyle and home-ware products in the UK. The buyers work with artisans throughout the world bringing stylish and beautiful furnishings back to their barn in Devon.

The barn is split into several different areas and is the perfect backdrop for the unique display of decorative goods. nkuku is an interior designer's dream and stocks everything from crockery to Indian cupboards. There is also a café with seating both inside and out in their courtyard, serving sharing platters, light lunches and decent coffee.

**ADDRESS**

Brockhills Barns

TQ9 7PS

**PHONE**

01803 465365

**NEAR HERE**

Timehouse Muzeum (p159)

Blackpool Sands (p25)

Rockfish (p65)

# No Guts No Glory

**SHOPPING** | **EXETER** | EX4 3JQ

No Guts No Glory is a utopia for those who love unique print and illustration. This little shop sells a carefully selected range of art prints, books, clothing, gifts and greeting cards. Founders Nathan and Hayley Maker designed a shop to feel like a home from home and personally select everything that is on offer in store.

The product criteria is that each item should be nourishing to the soul or pleasing to the eye. They also provide a bespoke picture framing service as well as small batch coffee from their coffee bar. Be sure to pop by for a boost of creative inspiration and some retail therapy.

## ADDRESS

125 Fore Street

EX4 3JQ

## PHONE

01392 757179

## NEAR HERE

Artigiano Exeter (p114)

The Exploding Bakery (p147)

Exeter Cathedral (p164)

# Quay Antiques Centre

**SHOPPING | TOPSHAM | EX3 0JB**

Topsham Quay Antiques Centre began life as a flour storage building and was transformed into a successful Antique emporium in 1992. This rustic interior is a treasure trove of interesting, eclectic and sometimes eccentric offerings.

Quay Antiques Centre is a collective made up of over 60 antique dealers. The space is large and set over three floors ensuring that the range of antiques on offer is vast and varied. Its riverside location makes the perfect tranquil backdrop for visitors to browse militaria, clocks, textiles, jewellery and so much more.

## ADDRESS

The Quay, Strand
EX3 0JB

## PHONE

01392 874006

## NEAR HERE

L'estuaire Restaurant Ltd (p88)
The Salutation Inn (p64)
Pig and Pallet (p87)

# Palmers Wine Store

**SHOPPING | BRIDPORT | DT6 4JA**

Palmers Wine Store is nestled into the banks of the river Brit and has been creating fine ales since 1794. Beautiful features from the original thatched buildings have been preserved including the waterwheel and high stone archway, which was originally built for traditional horse-drawn Brewery Drays.

With a focus on using the finest ingredients and methods instilled from the traditional brewing process, you can trace the ale from the grain and malt store to the sampling rooms with their insightful tours. At the end of the tour you can sample each reputable ale in this charming and independent brewery.

## ADDRESS

The Old Brewery,
West Bay Road
DT6 4JA

## PHONE

01308 422396

## NEAR HERE

The Bull (p94)
The Seaside House (p67)
The Station Kitchen (p78)

216

# The Country Store

**SHOPPING | KENTON | EX6 8JE**

The Country Store, besides Powderham Castle is home to five independent businesses. These include The Powderham Farm Shop with its collection of fresh local produce including meat and veg, Urban & Rural plants where you can spruce up your home and garden with a fantastic selection of flowers and botanicals and The Orangery restaurant for breakfasts, light lunches and pastries.

The Country Store is located besides the River Exe and is worth a stop-over when visiting the castle or before catching the ferry to Exmouth. The stores and restaurant look over the castle's deer park and grounds.

**ADDRESS**

Powderham Estate
EX6 8JE

**PHONE**

01626 891883

**NEAR HERE**

Powderham Castle (p15)
River Exe (p18)
The Salutation Inn (p64)

# Ryder & Hope

**SHOPPING | LYME REGIS | DT7 3QE**

Ryder & Hope is an interesting design led collaboration incorporating interiors, retail and online. The brand encompasses an interior design service that focuses on commercial properties as well as domestic spaces. Ryder & Hope Store is their first retail space, selecting products from designers and crafts people as well as finding pieces to inspire everyday living.

Ryder & Hope source beautiful home-wares and products chosen because of their design, heritage and usefulness. Iconic pieces sit alongside the traditional and hand-crafted with seasonal collections that reflect key trends.


**ADDRESS**

30 Broad Street

DT7 3QE

**PHONE**

01297 443304


**NEAR HERE**


Lyme Regis Harbour (p44)

Lyme Regis Brewery (p141)

The Harbour Inn (p47)

CHAPTER SEVEN

# FOOD SHOPS

# Stokeley

**FOOD SHOPS | KINGSBRIDGE | TQ7 2SE**

Stokeley Farm Shop and cafe, is a deli, butchery, restaurant cafe and plant centre, stocking everyday groceries and a wide selection of alcohol, including beer from their very own brewery. Their deli counter showcases high quality olives, charcuterie and award winning artisan cheeses, whilst their cafe incorporates their home-grown and home-baked produce into their flavoursome dishes.

Stokeley supports local producers and the local economy, sourcing products as locally as possible to minimise food miles and carbon footprints, whilst also growing their own fruit and vegetables throughout the year.

## ADDRESS

Stokeley Barton Farm
TQ7 2SE

## PHONE

01548 581605

## NEAR HERE

Sea Breeze (p72)
Start Point Lighthouse (p14)
Millbrook Inn (p48)

# Deli Rocks

**FOOD SHOPS | BOURNEMOUTH | BH6 3QS**

Deli Rocks is an Italian delicatessen, espresso bar and eatery, owned and run by Giovanni Dora. Born to Italian parents from Parma, Giovanni grew up immersed in the food culture associated with this city and developed Deli Rocks to create a deli with a vibrant atmosphere, serving the highest quality Italian produce.

All of the cheeses and meats are from award winning and reputable companies in Italy. The brick interior, dried chillis suspended from the ceiling and vast glass deli counter brimming with Italian produce, are highlighted with eccentric accessories.

## ADDRESS

23 Southbourne Grove
BH6 3QS

## PHONE

07920 746210

## NEAR HERE

James and White (p92)
Velo Domestique (p99)
Coffee and Dice (p102)

# Lyme Regis Brewery

**FOOD SHOPS | LYME REGIS | DT7 3PU**

Based at the historic old Town Mill in Lyme Regis, Lyme Regis Brewery create a range of five regular beers and some additional seasonal specials, all of which have won the coveted 'Taste of The West' award. They are all hand-made in small batches by their master brewer, using only the finest natural ingredients.

Lyme Regis Bewery use locally-sourced ingredients wherever possible. Visit them and try their beers on draught. Sit outside in The Town Mill's historic cobbled courtyard with a pint or two and watch the world go by. Their shop on site sells the full range of bottled beers and local ciders.

## ADDRESS

Mill Lane

DT7 3PU

## PHONE

01297 444354

## NEAR HERE

Ryder & Hope (p137)

Lyme Regis Harbour (p44)

The Bull (p94)

# Cove Fish

**FOOD SHOPS | WEST LULWORTH | BH20 5RQ**

Nestled under the cliffs and set back from the shingle shore of Lulworth Cove, fish doesn't come much fresher than the catch at Cove Fish. Straight from their boat, mere metres from their unassuming shed shop, this family run business has been situated in the picturesque Lulworth Cove for generations.

Ideal for BBQs, campers or simply those with a passion for fresh, locally harvested fish. Crab, lobster, scallops and an enviable range of fish are available to buy from their knowledgeable staff. Chalk boards detail the catch-of-the-day and their scallops are particularly popular.

## ADDRESS

Main Road
BH20 5RQ

## PHONE

01929 400807

## NEAR HERE

Lulworth Cove (p43)
Durdle Door (p12)
Corfe Castle (p168)

# Duck's Farmshop & Café

**FOOD SHOPS | WEYMOUTH | DT3 4HG**

Duck's Farmshop is a cafe and large country food shop and delicatessen selling a fusion of local farm produce and established brands. Regional cheeses and breads are served from the deli counter alongside cured meats and vegetables in this airy and contemporary store.

The coffee bar with its white brick tiles and wooden counter serving baked goods, is popular with cyclists and campers visiting the area and the store is renowned for their breakfasts. Fully licensed and serving food throughout the day, the shop is a convenient stop-off destination.

## ADDRESS

Bramdon Lane

DT3 4HG

## PHONE

01305 534111

## NEAR HERE

Abbotsbury Subtropical Gardens (p24)

Finca (p107)

Crab House café (93)

# @ the bakery

**FOOD SHOPS | FROGMORE | TQ7 2NT**

Having been awarded 2 and 3 Gold Stars at The Great Taste Awards '@ the bakery' create artisan breads early each morning, along with pastries, warm pasties and quiches, using locally sourced ingredients.

Their marmalade and whiskey bread pudding is a unique and popular choice as are their award-winning tray bakes and Victoria sponge. @ the bakery also stock basics from milk, butter, free range eggs, and newspapers alongside an increasing range of deli products and local handmade preserves.

## ADDRESS

Kingsbridge
TQ7 2NT

## PHONE

01548 531236

## NEAR HERE

The Crabshell Inn (p56)
Millbrook Inn (p48)
The Pantry (p148)

# Exploding Bakery Exeter

**FOOD SHOPS | EXETER | EX4 3SB**

Bakers Tom Oxford & Oliver Coysh are renowned for their passionate and innovative approach to creating flavour and texture, Exploding Bakery is dedicated to baking handmade cakes with complex flavours, using simple, local ingredients, and no junk. Watch the bakers at work in their cosy café next door.

The parquet flooring, dark grey and white interior and eclectic furniture feature against a backdrop of rustic shelves stacked with brown paper bags, brimming with delicious artisanal coffee and milled maize. Try their delicious selection of handmade cakes or the soup with their hand-baked soda bread.

**ADDRESS**

3a Queen Street
EX4 3SB

**PHONE**

01392 427900

**NEAR HERE**

Exeter Cathedral (p164)
Royal Albert Museum (p165)
Artigiano Exeter (p114)

# The Pantry

**FOOD SHOPS | KINGSBRIDGE | TQ7 1HU**

The Pantry is owned by two sisters with a passion for quality food. The delicatessen is also home to a popular coffee shop where you can find the best morning wake-up. Their counter is stacked full of home-cooked produce from sausage rolls and pork pies to Mediterranean antipasti and fresh salads.

Try their indulgent chocolate-chip banana bread with natural yogurt and honey or their milkshakes which look like something out of a 1950s American diner. Sumptuous gift hampers, stacked with cheese, biscuits, wine and hams can be arranged. The Pantry is everything you wished yours was.

**ADDRESS**

1 Duke Street

TQ7 1HU

**PHONE**

01548 856100

**NEAR HERE**

Millbrook Inn (p48)

Stokeley (p139)

@ The Bakery (p146)

# Framptons

**FOOD SHOPS | BRIDPORT | DT6 3LF**

Framptons of Bridport is located in Market House, where butchers have reportedly been working on the site for 750 years. Many historic features of the building are evident in the traditional shop interior.

Framptons itself was started in 1993 by Phil Frampton, and the family business has been serving the town of Bridport ever since. Quality is at the heart of everything that Framptons produce and they provide their meat for both retail customers and respected local restaurants.


**ADDRESS**

Market House, East Street

DT6 3LF

**PHONE**

01308 422995


**NEAR HERE**


The Bull (p94)

The Station Kitchen (p78)

The Seaside House (p67)

# The Bake House

**FOOD SHOPS | SALCOMBE | TQ8 8BY**

The Bake House in Salcombe has been creating authentic, hand crafted baked goods since 1973. Everything is made from scratch on a daily basis using uncompromisingly good quality ingredients.

French techniques are combined with traditional British baking methods to create a variety of artisan breads, baguettes and pastries. 'Best sellers' come in the form of sugar dusted doughnuts, carrot cakes and sourdough loafs. You can also park outside which is rather a rarity for Salcombe.

## ADDRESS

3 Fore Street
TQ8 8BY

## PHONE

01548 842824

## NEAR HERE

The Winking Prawn (p85)
Sailor V Salcombe (p120)
The Ferry Inn (p50)

# Le Petit Prince

**FOOD SHOPS | BOURNEMOUTH | BH4 9EP**

Le Petit Prince is a family run patisserie based in Westbourne, Bournemouth, using local Dorset ingredients to make and supply the finest quality produce, from their award winning breads to their highly sought after cakes and viennoiserie.

The counter at Le Petit Prince is piled high with hand-baked loaves from rustic granary and sourdough to cinnamon butter twist. The interior is rustic, with an exposed brick wall, stripped wooden floors, industrial lighting and a glass counter full of indulgent cakes and patisseries.

## ADDRESS

48 Poole Road
BH4 9EP

## PHONE

01202 989874

## NEAR HERE

Bermuda (p103)
South Coast Roast (p124)
Coffee and Dice (p102)

# Delicious

**FOOD SHOPS | WEYMOUTH | DT4 8BZ**

An independent, family run delicatessen and wine merchant with a passion for locally sourced, award winning and homemade produce, selected from suppliers reflecting an equally impassioned food philosophy. Their wines are selected from independent vineyards to bring unique, affordable wines to their customers.

Situated on St.Alban Street in Weymouth, the delicatessen has a relaxed ambience. Renowned for their cheese boards which showcase the best of Dorset's produce, they are best enjoyed with a glass of their curated wine. Organic coffee and Rainforest Alliance teas are served alongside delicious cakes.

**ADDRESS**

23 St Alban Street

DT4 8BZ

**PHONE**

01305 789033

**NEAR HERE**

The Monkey's Fist (p96)

Il Porto (p95)

Duck's Farmshop & café (p143)

CHAPTER EIGHT

# CULTURE

# St Nicholas Chapel

**CULTURE | ILFRACOMBE | EX34 9EQ**

St Nicholas Chapel was built in 1321 by monks to keep the ancient mariners safe from crashing on to the rocks on the north Devon coast, using the lighthouse to help guide the way. As well as a working lighthouse, St Nicholas Chapel was also built as a place of worship for the people of Ilfracombe.

The chapel today is regarded as an iconic landmark overlooking the harbour where the occasional services are held. St Nicholas Chapel has stunning 360 degree views of the surrounding countryside and coastline and is steeped in fascinating history.

**ADDRESS**

The Quay
EX34 9EQ

**PHONE**

N/A

**NEAR HERE**

The Quay Restaurant (p83)
Annie and the Flint (p115)
Stoned (p82)

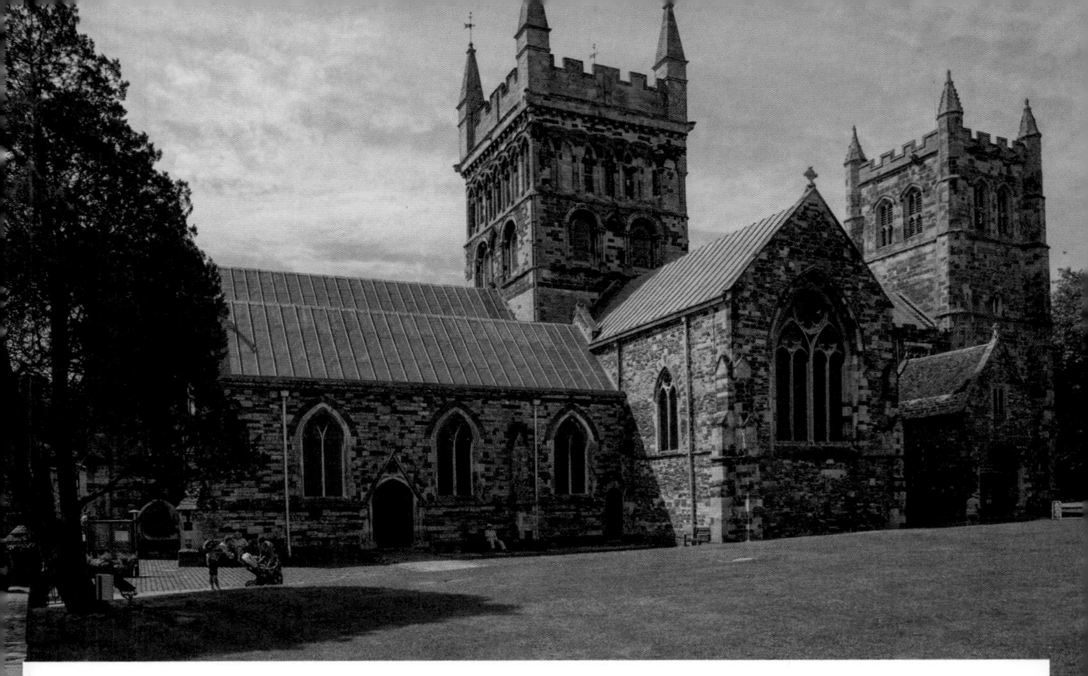

# Wimborne Minster and Chained Library

**CULTURE** | **WIMBORNE** | BH21 1HT

Wimbourne Minster has been a place of worship and prayer for over 1300 years and its two great towers can be seen from any approach to the town. Look out for the Quarter Jack statue on the West tower, installed in 1612, Jack strikes two bells every quarter hour.

There are many fascinating features in the church, the most notable being one of the worlds five chained libraries. The library is located above the choir vestry and is reached via a spiral staircase, it showcases a collection of over 400 ancient books of great import, which were chained to poles within the room to be enjoyed without removal.

**ADDRESS**

High Street
BH21 1HT

**PHONE**

01202 884753

**NEAR HERE**

The Tickled Pig (p76)
The Thirsty Bird (p104)
Yellow Bicycle café (p128)

# Torre Abbey

**CULTURE | TORQUAY | TQ2 5JE**

Torre Abbey, established in 1196, is a museum of history and art housed in an Ancient Scheduled Monument on the beautiful South Devon coast. Founded as a monastery for Premonstratensian canons, it is now considered the best-preserved medieval monastery in Devon and Cornwall.

Torre Abbey is renowned for its art collection, regular exhibitions and tranquil walled gardens containing a multitude of exotic plants. This natural haven is beautiful and perfect for walking or picnicking. The Torre Abbey Tearooms offer coffee and an assortment of light meals and cakes.

## ADDRESS

The King's Drive

TQ2 5JE

## PHONE

01803 293593

## NEAR HERE

Timehouse Muzeum (p159)

nkuku Lifestyle Store (p130)

Riverford Field Kitchen (p74)

# Timehouse Muzeum

**CULTURE | TOTNES | TQ9 5NJ**

The Timehouse Muzeum is a unique Narnia world, created and funded by local artist and designer Julie Lafferty. Four floors take you on a colourful journey through time in an 18th century listed building in the heart of Totnes.

It's hard to imagine the transformed dream-space behind the main streets storefront, but it's worth getting lost in. Several rooms display and exhibit different historic events using unusual decorations and artifacts; making this an eccentric and quirky museum to visit.

**ADDRESS**

69 Fore Street
TQ9 5NJ

**PHONE**

01803 862109

**NEAR HERE**

nkuku Lifestyle Store (p130)
Riverford Field Kitchen (p74)
Torre Abbey (p158)

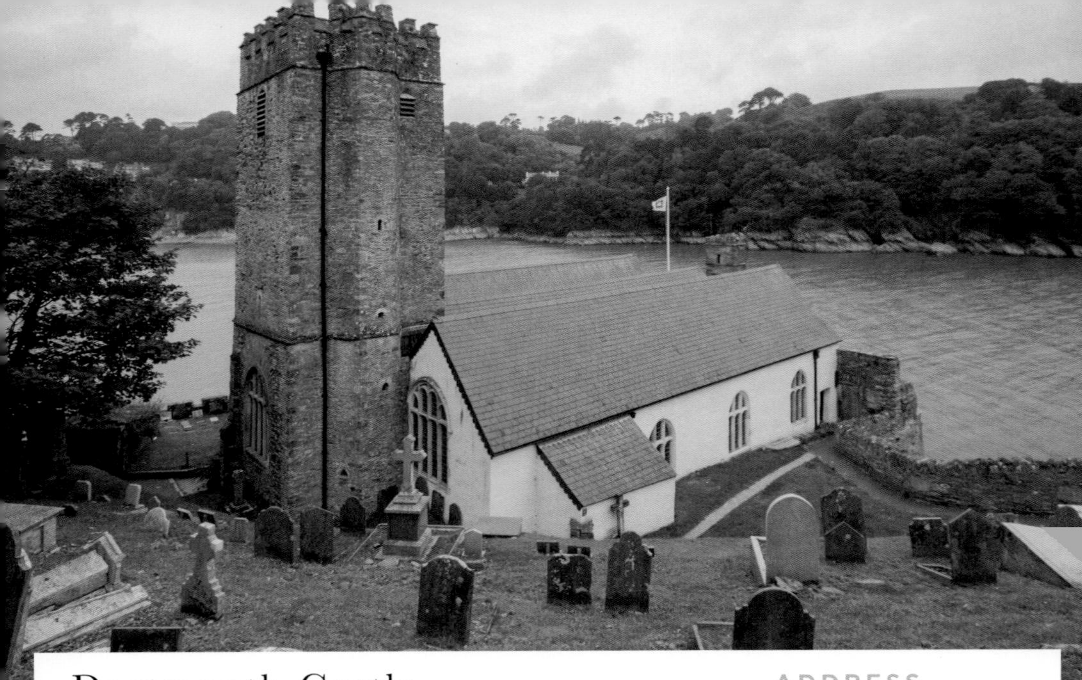

# Dartmouth Castle

**CULTURE | DARTMOUTH | TQ6 0JN**

Be inspired by Dartmouth's amazing history by visiting Dartmouth Castle in the most scenic position on the water's edge of the river Dart. Arrive in style along the river or you can walk from the town and take in the wonderful views. The castle has acted as a fortress for over 600 years, guarding the entrance to the narrow Estuary.

An array of heavy artillery is on display, giving the visitor an impression of how the castle operated. You can climb up the gun-tower for incredible views over the river and after your visit, there are plenty of options for lunch in nearby Dartmouth.

## ADDRESS

Castle Road
TQ6 0JN

## PHONE

0370 3331181

## NEAR HERE

Blackpool Sands (p25)
Dartmouth (p34)
Rockfish (p65)

# The Golden Hind

**CULTURE** | **BRIXHAM** | TQ5 8AW

Originally built in 1963 for BBC filming purposes, The Golden Hind Museum Ship is now a permanently anchored feature of Brixham Harbour. The Golden Hind is a replica of the original ship that belonged to the famous navigator Sir Francis Drake. The ship remains an accurate representation of life on board an Elizabethan ship in the age of exploration.

Sir Francis Drake is best remembered as an explorer. In his most famous ship, the Golden Hind, Drake became the first Englishman to circumnavigate the globe in an epic expedition of plunder and discovery over 435 years ago, covering over 360,000 miles.

## ADDRESS

The Quay
TQ5 8AW

## PHONE

01803 856223

## NEAR HERE

Breakwater Coffee Shop (p69)
Brixham Harbour (p30)
Port Espresso (p116)

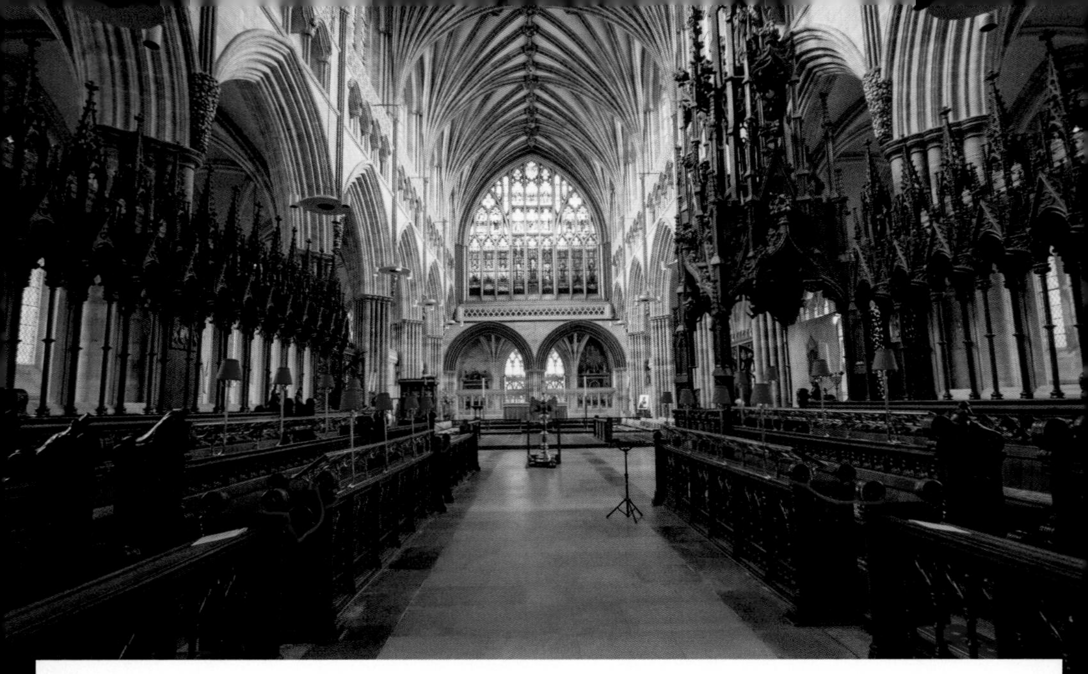

# Exeter Cathedral

**CULTURE | EXETER | EX1 1HS**

Exeter Cathedral is an Anglican cathedral and the seat of the Bishop of Exeter. Built between 1112-1400, the Cathedral is a stunning example of Gothic architecture and an immense amount of skill and craftsmanship is evident. It has the longest uninterrupted gothic vaulted ceiling in the world, two Norman towers and impressive front carvings.

It is home to some fascinating artifacts; including the Exeter Cathedral Astronomical Clock and a library containing the Exeter Book of Anglo-Saxon Poetry. The cathedral remains today an active parish, and is prevalent in its surrounding community.

## ADDRESS

1 The Cloisters

EX1 1HS

## PHONE

01392 255573

## NEAR HERE

Pig and Pallet (p87)

Mangos café (p109)

Royal Albert Memorial Museum (p165)

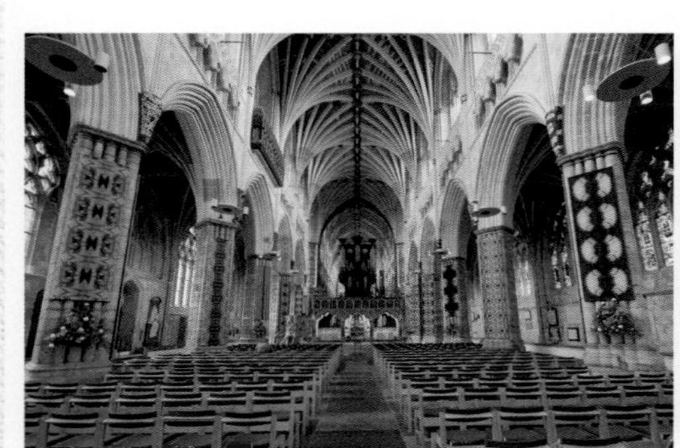

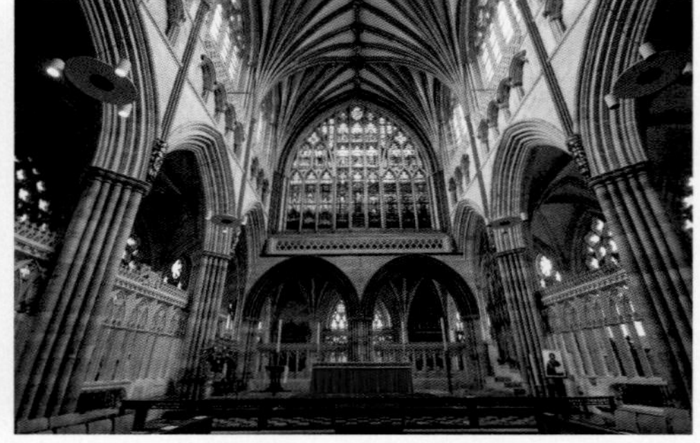

# Royal Albert Memorial Museum

**CULTURE** | **EXETER** | EX4 3RX

The Royal Albert Memorial Museum holds a diverse collection of over 1 million objects including examples of zoology, anthropology, fine art, local and overseas archaeology.

Founded in 1868, the museum is housed in a Gothic Revival building that has undergone several extensions during its history. The museum was re-opened in December 2011 after a redevelopment lasting four years and costing £24M. Since its re-opening the museum has received several awards including "Museum of the Year" by The Art Fund charity in 2012. The museum is open 10am to 5pm every day except Mondays and bank holidays. Entry is free.

## ADDRESS

Queen Street

EX4 3RX

## PHONE

01392 265 858

## NEAR HERE

The Exploding Bakery (p147)

Artigiano Exeter (p114)

No Guts No Glory (p131)

# Christchurch Priory Church

**CULTURE | CHRISTCHURCH | BH23 1BU**

Building of Christchurch Priory Church began in 1094 when Ranulf Flambard, a chief minister of King William II decided to knock down 9 smaller churches in the surrounding area and create one large central place of worship.

When the church was being built, carpenters failed to cut the right size beam. Overnight, a mysterious carpenter visited and by morning that same beam was miraculously the right size. Many believed that the carpenter was Jesus Christ and this is how the town changed its name from Thuinam to the present day Christchurch. It is the longest parish church in the country and is larger than 21 English Anglican Cathedrals.

**ADDRESS**

Quay Road
BH23 1BU

**PHONE**

01202 485804

**NEAR HERE**

James and White (p92)
Velo Domestique (p99)
Deli Rocks (p140)

# Northe Fort

**CULTURE** | **WEYMOUTH** | DT4 8UF

Northe Fort stands proud at the entrance to Weymouth Harbour and was built by the Victorians to protect Portland Harbour. A visit to the Fort gives you an interesting understanding of how it was manned and worked as a means of defence.

Constructed over three levels the Northe Fort displays and exhibits an underground labyrinth of passageways, gun decks and information about the advances of wartime technology. The Fort also offers stunning views over the Jurassic Coast and Weymouth. Be careful in the dark as it's rumoured to be haunted.

**ADDRESS**

Barrack Road

DT4 8UF

**PHONE**

01305 766626

**NEAR HERE**

Delicious (p154)

Weymouth (p41)

The Monkey's Fist (p96)

# Corfe Castle

**CULTURE** | **WAREHAM** | **BH20 5EZ**

Guarding the principal route through the Purbeck Hills, the 1000 year old Corfe Castle's dramatic remains stand in an elevated position as a representation of its colourful and significant history. The tumbledown, moss embellished walls and rugged beauty conceal its diverse and often turbulent past.

From a Saxon stronghold and Normal fortress to a royal palace, the castle and town are steeped in history. The National Trust are now responsible for the castle and have created an educational environment with information points. A licensed tea room and garden offer refreshment and a small shop sells gifts.

## ADDRESS

The Square, Corfe Castle
BH20 5EZ

## PHONE

01929 481294

## NEAR HERE

Swanage (p42)

Java Independent Coffee House (p125)

Love Cake (p127)

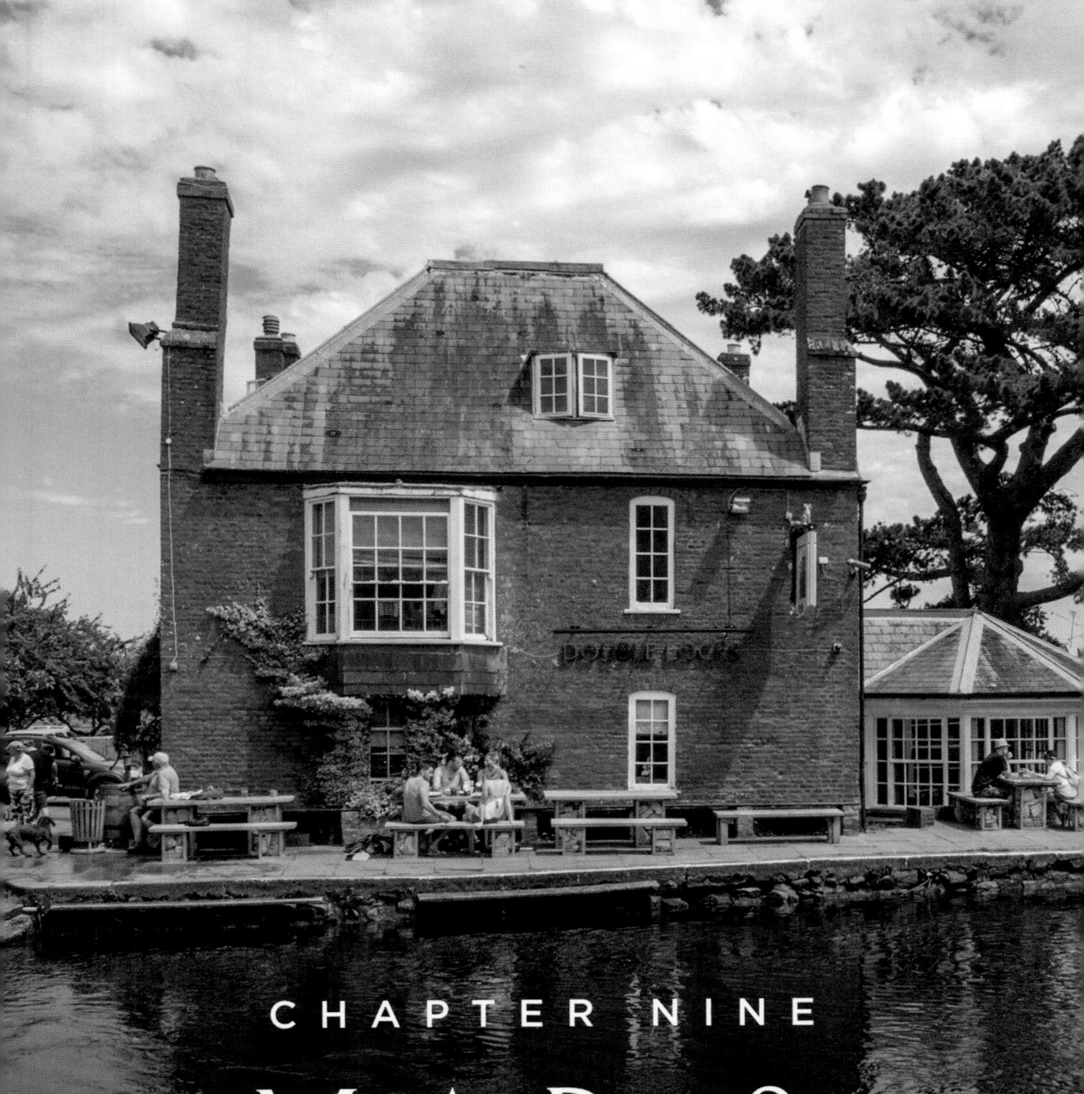

CHAPTER NINE

# MAP & INDEX

# INDEX

# Notes

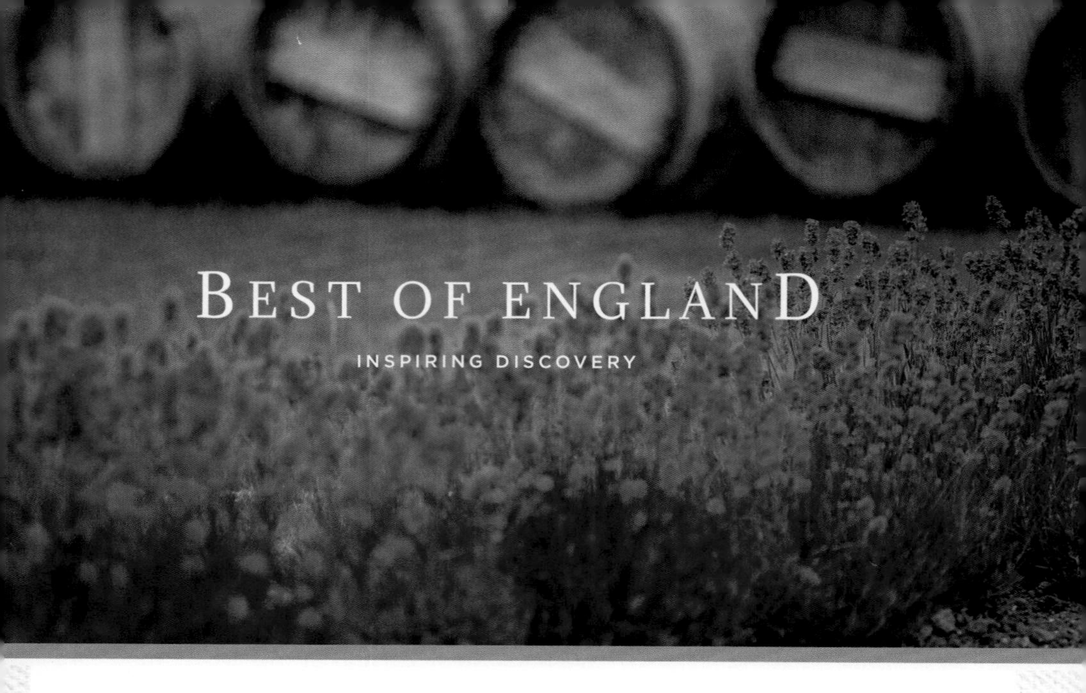


# About Best of England

Honest Recommendations & Hidden Gems

### What is Best of England?

Best of England is a curated collection of travel recommendations. Each one is researched and has been visited and photographed by a member of the Best of England team.

### Authenticity & integrity

None of the businesses in this travel guide have paid to be included and we visit every business that we recommend. This guide is based on our own experiences and opinions. We think honesty is a really important part of what we are trying to achieve.

### Local knowledge is key

We believe there is nothing better than local knowledge. That's why we speak to the people that live there to find out where to go.

### Quality is everything

Quality is behind everything we do and we will never compromise on the recommendations we make. We worry about the details from the thickness of the paper to the size of each font we use and we hope that this effort is reflected in the quality of our products.

### Great content comes first

We use our photography to tell a story for each of the businesses we recommend. We want to bring each one to life and inspire our readers to visit themselves.

### Tell us what you think

We are always on the look out for ways to improve. Feedback is really important to us in order to make the best product possible. If you have any suggestions or feedback then please let us know via email to **info@bestofengland.com**

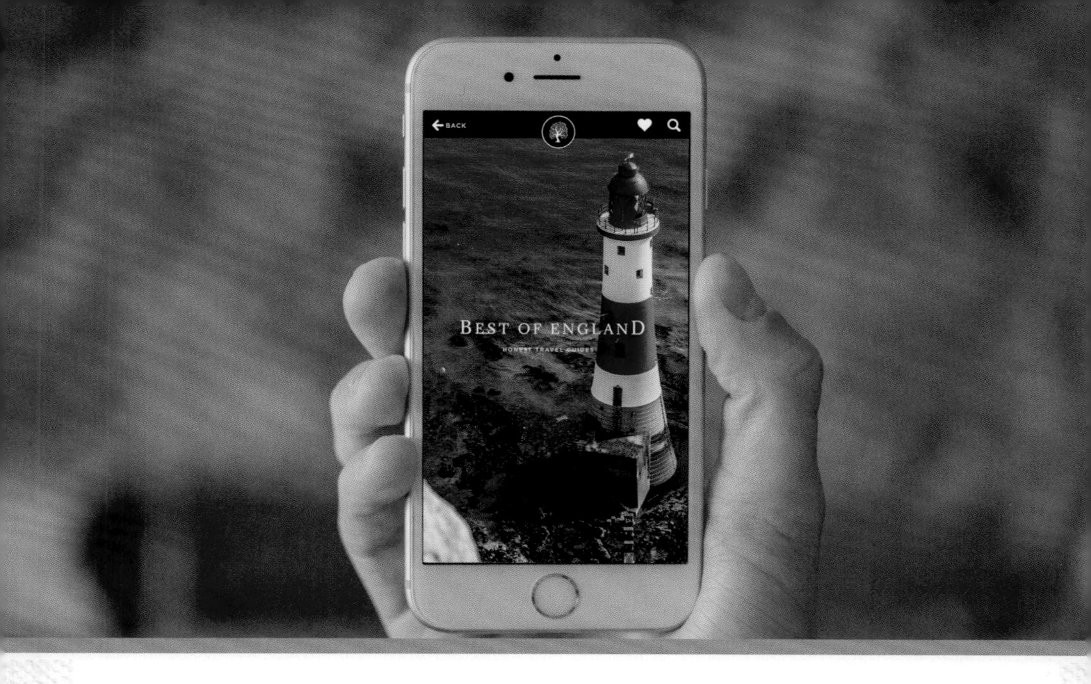
BACK
BEST OF ENGLAND

ISLE OF WIGHT & HAMPSHIRE
DEVON & DORSET
EAST ANGLIA
CORNWALL
LONDON
LAKE DISTRICT
YORKSHIRE
KENT
SUSSEX

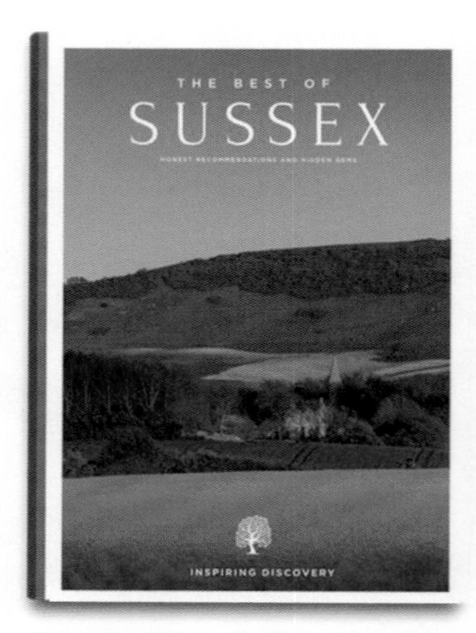


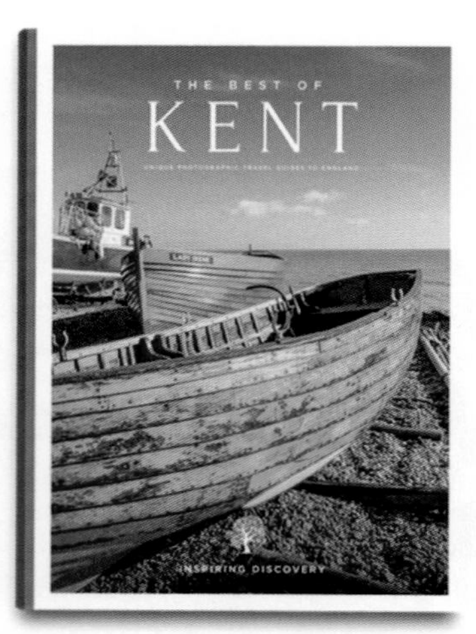


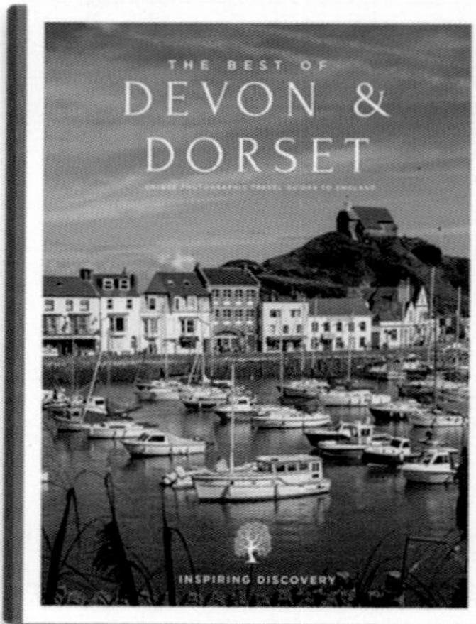


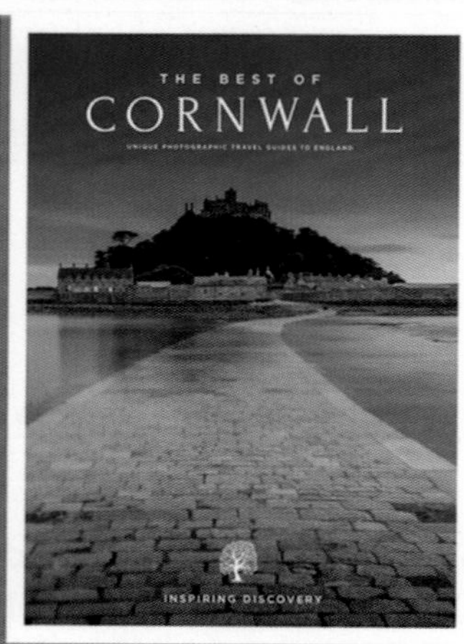


# Meet the family

Honest Recommendations & Hidden Gems

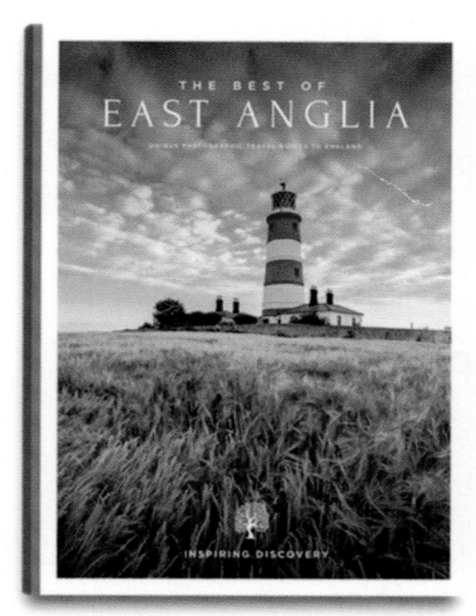
THE BEST OF
EAST ANGLIA
INSPIRING DISCOVERY

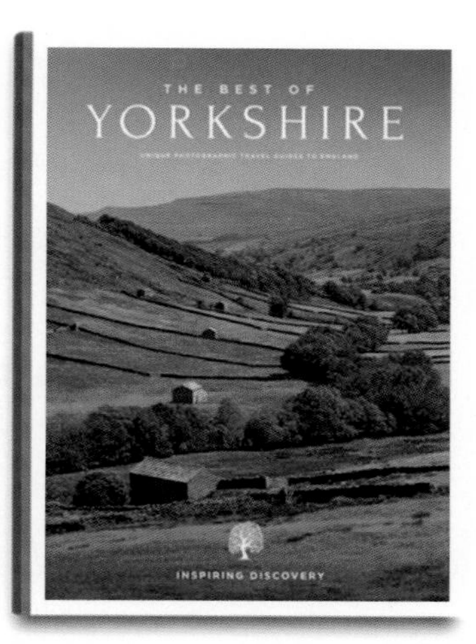
THE BEST OF
YORKSHIRE
INSPIRING DISCOVERY

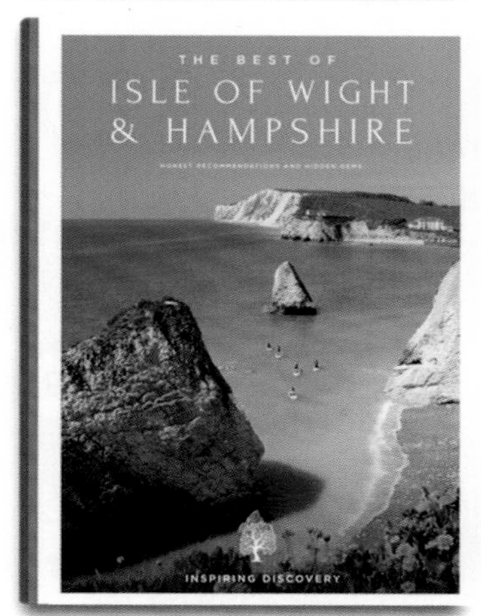
THE BEST OF
ISLE OF WIGHT
& HAMPSHIRE
INSPIRING DISCOVERY

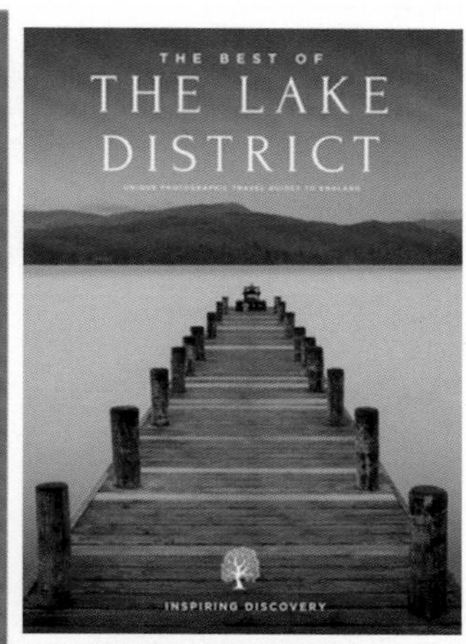
THE BEST OF
THE LAKE
DISTRICT
INSPIRING DISCOVERY

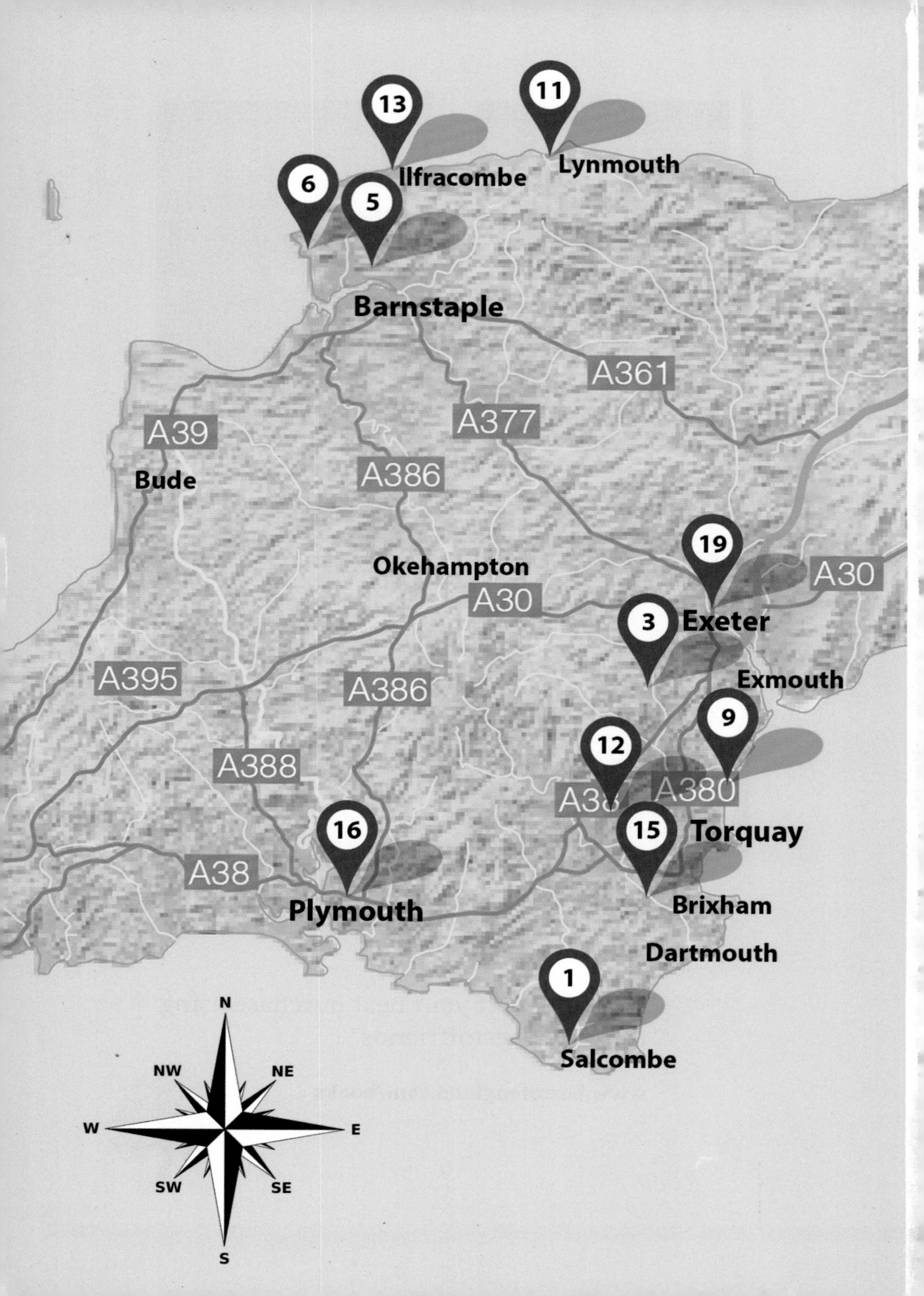
13
11
Ilfracombe
Lynmouth
6
5
Barnstaple
A361
A377
A39
A386
Bude
19
Okehampton
A30
A30
3
Exeter
A395
A386
Exmouth
9
12
A388
A380
16
15
Torquay
A38
Plymouth
Brixham
Dartmouth
1
Salcombe
N
NW
NE
W
E
SW
SE
S